河姆渡文化精粹

启功题签

主　编　叶树望
撰　文　黄渭金　王凌浩　赵晓波
　　　　熊巨龙　姚晓强
摄　影　郑　华　孙之常
英　译　曹　楠
日　译　后藤健
编　务　王凌浩　黄渭金　郑　红

Editor-in-chief: Ye Shuwang
Authors: Huang Weijin　Wang Linghao　Zhao Xiaobo
Xiong Julong　Yao Xiaoqiang
Photographer: Zheng Hua　Sun Zhichang
English translator: Cao Nan
Japanese translator: Goto Ken
Edit manager: Wang Linghao　Huang Weijin　Zheng Hong

主　編　葉樹望
撰　文　黄渭金　王凌浩　趙暁波
　　　　熊巨龍　姚暁強
撮　影　鄭　華　孫之常
英　訳　曹　楠
日　訳　後藤健
編　務　王凌浩　黄渭金　鄭　紅

河姆渡文化精粹

文物出版社

封面题签　启　功
封面设计　周小玮
责任编辑　谷艳雪
责任印制　王少华

图书在版编目（CIP）数据

河姆渡文化精粹/河姆渡遗址博物馆编．—北京：文物出版社，2002.12
ISBN 7-5010-1352-7

Ⅰ．河…　Ⅱ．河…　Ⅲ．新石器时代文化-文化遗址-余姚市-图录　Ⅳ．K873.553.2

中国版本图书馆 CIP 数据核字（2002）第 037844 号

河姆渡文化精粹

河姆渡遗址博物馆

*

文 物 出 版 社 出 版 发 行

北京五四大街 29 号

http://www.wenwu.com

E-mail:web@wenwu.com

北京国彩印刷有限公司印刷

新　华　书　店　经　销

889×1194　1/16　印张：13.5

2002 年 12 月第一版　2002 年 12 月第一次印刷

ISBN 7-5010-1352-7/K·600　定价：200.00 元

Gems of the Hemudu Culture
河姆渡文化精粹

The Museum of the Hemudu Site
河姆渡遺址博物館　編

Cultural Relics Publishing House
文物出版社

目　　录
Contents
目　　録

图版目录

玉石器

骨、角、牙器

木　器

陶　器

木构遗迹

动植物遗存及其他

List of Plates

Jade, Stone Artifacts

Bone, Antler, Ivory, Tooth Artifacts

Wooden Implements

Pottery Wares

Remains of Wooden Structure

Remains of Animals, Plants and Others

図版目録

玉石器

骨、角、牙器

木　器

土　器

木造建築

動、植物遺存体及びその他

序

河姆渡文化因河姆渡遗址而得名，迄今已知宁绍平原及舟山群岛一带遍布她的足迹。木构干栏式建筑、造型新颖的夹炭陶器、石器、木器、骨器及象牙雕刻制品和丰富的动植物遗存等构成了河姆渡文化独特的面貌。河姆渡遗址的发现，改变了人们对长江流域新石器文化的偏见，冲击了只有黄河流域才是中华远古文化摇篮的传统观念。河姆渡文化已成为中华远古文明历史的见证而编入历史教科书。

中国自古以来就是个农业大国，原始农业的发生、兴起、发展在中华远古文化的形成和发展进程中曾起过巨大作用，也为后来的中华文明奠定了基础。20 多年前河姆渡遗址发现公元前 5000 年左右的丰富的稻作遗存，震撼了学术界，表明了长江下游地区在距今 7000 年前后就拥有发达的稻作农业，为丁颖先生的中国栽培稻起源于本土的理论提供了佐证，促使人们把稻作起源中心的关注焦点逐渐从南亚转移到古老的中国，掀起了中国稻作起源研究的热潮。

继 20 世纪 70 年代河姆渡遗址两次大规模发掘以来，90 年代河姆渡文化遗址的考古发掘接二连三地在宁绍平原展开，并获得了累累硕果。丰富多彩的物质遗存是这一文化物化形式的载体，是我们探求中华远古文化重要发源地之一的直观、形象、生动的不可再生的文物资源，它们传递着六七千年前河姆渡人的物质生活和精神生活的种种信息，让现今的人们对祖先活动的奥秘遐想联翩，令多少学人为她倾注了无数的笔墨与辛劳，又令多少人为之折服倾倒。

一次好的机遇使我与余姚河姆渡遗址结下了不解之缘，在那里一待便是 10 个年头，长年与之晤对凝思，培育了一种特殊的感情，当河姆渡遗址博物馆馆长告诉我欲出版一本《河姆渡文化精粹》时，我的兴奋之情难以言表。明年是河姆渡遗址发现发掘 30 周年，编辑出版这样一本图录，展示近 30 年以来河姆渡文化考古新发现，无疑具有特殊的纪念意义，对于宣传河姆渡文化、深入研究河姆渡文化必将起着推动和促进作用。这些年来，河姆渡遗址博物馆的同仁们，坚持致力于河姆渡文化展示宣传的探索与研究，在陈列讲解上开拓创新，赢得了观众。奉献给大家的《河姆渡文化精粹》不仅能给您带来艺术的享受，更重要的是这本图录能成为您了解河姆渡文化的窗口，成为引领您进入远古河姆渡人生活的朋友。

是为序。

刘　军

2002 年 1 月

Preface

The Hemudu culture is named after the discovery of the Hemudu site. To present, it is found all over the Ningbo-Shaoxing Plains and Zhoushan Islands. The wooden pile structure, carbon tempered pottery in a novel stage, stone, wooden, bone wares and ivory carvings and rich faunal and botany remains make the Hemudu culture distinct. The discovery of the Hemudu site changed prejudice against the Neolithic cultures at the Yangtze River valley, and is pounding at the traditional view that only the Yellow River valley is the cradle of ancient Chinese culture. The Hemudu culture has become the witness of ancient Chinese civilization and is compiled into historical textbooks.

China has been a great nation of agriculture since antiquity. The origin, rise and development of primitive agriculture have played tremendous role in the formation and development of ancient Chinese culture, and also lay foundation for the formation of Chinese civilization. One score years ago, rich rice remains dated to 5,000 BC was recovered at the Hemudu site, which indicates that the people had already engaged in rice farming of a fairly advance level in the lower Yangtze River valley in c.7,000 BP. This discovery furnished evidences for Prof. Ding Ying's theory that the domesticated rice in China is originated in native land, pushes professionals transfer the focus of center of rice origin from the south Asia to China, and sets off a mass upsurge of the research into the origin of rice in China.

Following two large scaled excavations of the Hemudu site in 1970s, archaeological excavations of the Hemudu cultural sites were carried out in the Ningbo-Shaoxing Plains one after another in 1990s, and reaped rich fruits. The rich and varied material remains are carriers of the Hemudu culture, and also the un-reproductive antiquity resources of research into one of the birthplaces of ancient Chinese culture. They transmit messages of material and spiritual life of the Hemudu inhabitants in c.6,000-7,000 BP, and induce fantastic reveries about the secret of our ancestor. She made many scholars dedicated their endless efforts and writings to her, and overwhelmed with admiration for her, too.

I was irrevocably committed to the Hemudu site by a good opportunity, and had stayed there for 10 years. I have brought up special feelings with her during long time face-to-face and meditation. When the director of the Museum of the Hemudu Site told me that the volume of *Gems of the Hemudu Culture* would be compiled, I was so excited that there were no words can express my feeling. The next year is the 30th anniversary of the discovery and excavation of the Hemudu site, it has special meaning to compile this catalogue and exhibit the new archaeological finds of the Hemudu culture in the latest 30 years. It will greatly push and promote wide publicity and further studies of the Hemudu culture.

My colleagues worked in the Museum of the Hemudu Site devote much efforts to research how to exhibit and publicize the Hemudu culture, and they have brazen new trails and gained audience. The present volume not only let readers appreciate art of the Hemudu culture, but also is a window to comprehend the Hemudu culture and a friend leading you enter the life of the ancient Hemudu inhabitants.

Liu Jun
Jan, 2002

序

河姆渡文化の名称は河姆渡遺跡により命名され、これまでに寧紹平原および舟山群島一帯にあまねくその足跡が確認されている。木造高床式建築や斬新な造形の夾炭陶、石器、木器、骨器および象牙彫刻品や豊富な動植物遺存体など、独特な文化的特徴をもっている。河姆渡遺跡の発見は長江流域の新石器文化に対する偏見を改め、黄河流域のみが中国古代文化の揺籃の地であるという伝統的観点に衝撃を与えた。河姆渡文化は中国古代文明の歴史の証拠としてすでに歴史教科書でも取り扱われている。

中国は古来より農業大国であり、初期農耕の起源と発達は中国古代文化の形成と発展の過程において大きな役割を果たし、さらに後の中国文明の基礎となった。20 年前、河姆渡遺跡では紀元前 5000 年前後の稲作に関する豊富な証拠が発見され、長江下流域で7000 年前には稲作農耕が発達していたことが明らかになり、学術界を震撼させた。それは丁穎先生の中国栽培稲本土起源説の証拠となり、稲作起源に関する主な関心は次第に南アジアから古代中国へと移り、中国稲作起源の研究を高揚させることになった。

1970 年代の河姆渡遺跡の2 度にわたる大規模な発掘に続き、1990 年代には寧紹平原において河姆渡文化に属する遺跡の発掘が次々に実施され、多くの成果を得た。豊富な遺物はこの文化の内容を現代に伝えるものであり、我々が探し求める中国古代文化の重要な起源地の一つにおける直観的、形象的で生き生きとしたまたとない文化遺産である。これらは6000～7000 年前の河姆渡人の物質文化・精神文化に関する様々な情報を伝えるものであり、現在の人々に祖先の生活の奥深さに思いを馳せさせ、多くの研究者は河姆渡文化に対し苦労を重ねて筆を連ね、また多くの人を感嘆させる。

私が不思議な縁により河姆渡遺跡と関わる機会を得てから、すでに10 年の歳月が過ぎた。長年思いを凝らし、特別な感情が育くまれ、そして河姆渡遺址博物館の館長に『河姆渡文化精粋』を出版したいと告げられたとき、私の興奮は言葉では言い表しがたいものだった。来年には河姆渡遺跡は発見および発掘 30 周年を迎える。このような図録を出版し、この30 年間の河姆渡文化に関する考古新発見の展示を行うことは、間違いなく特別な記念的意義がある。そしてさらに河姆渡文化が宣伝され、研究を深めていくことだろう。ここ数年、河姆渡遺址博物館の同僚達は河姆渡文化の展示、宣伝の探索と研究に尽力してきた。そして展覧の解説に新機軸を打ち出し、観客を得ることに成功した。この度の『河姆渡文化精粋』は芸術的な享受をもたらすだけでなく、さらに重要なことはこの図録が河姆渡文化を理解するための窓口となり、読者が古代河姆渡人の生活の朋友となってくれることであろう。

これをもって序とする。

劉軍

2002 年 1 月

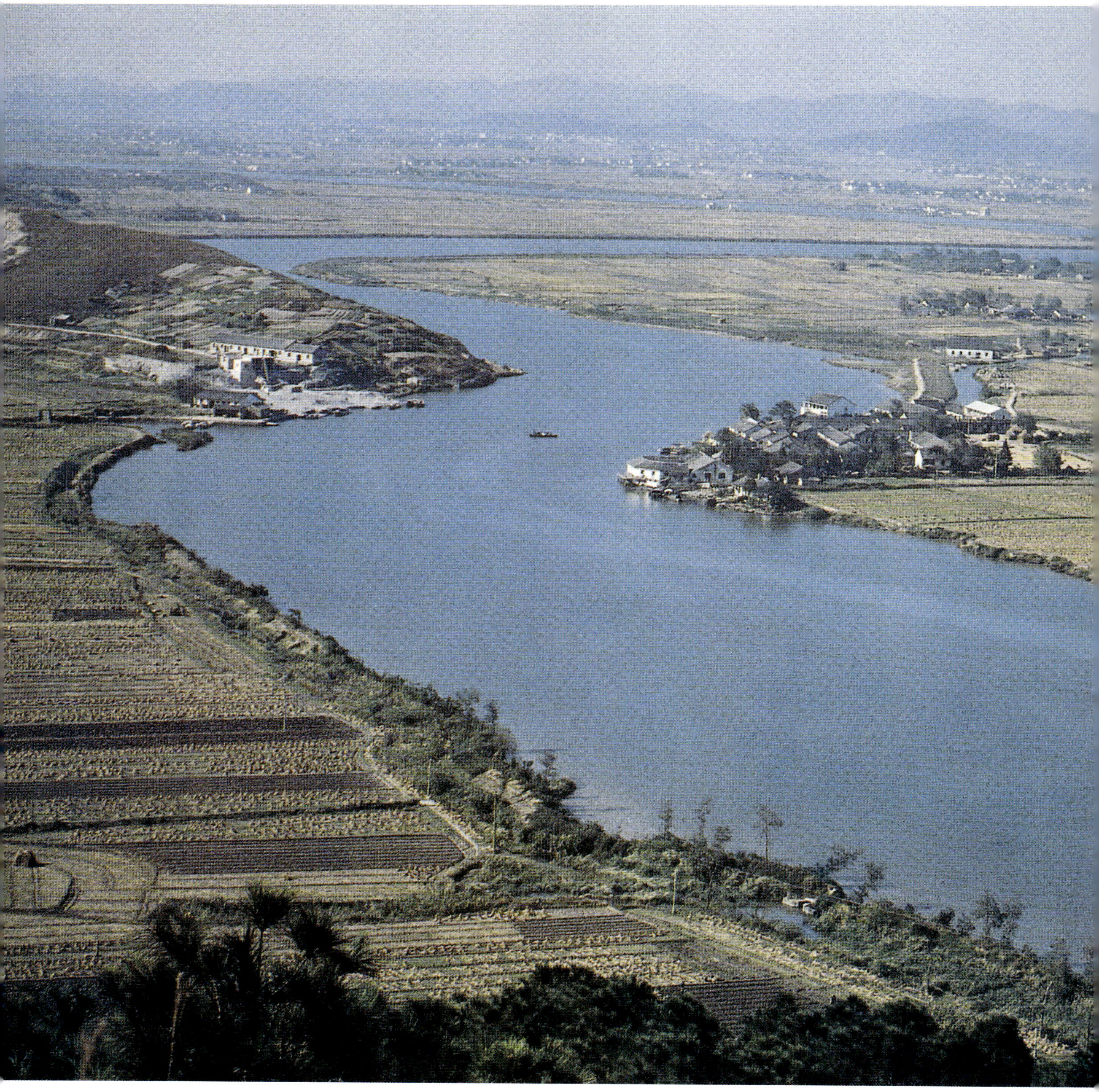

河姆渡遗址俯瞰
Overlook of the Hemudu site
河姆渡遺跡俯瞰

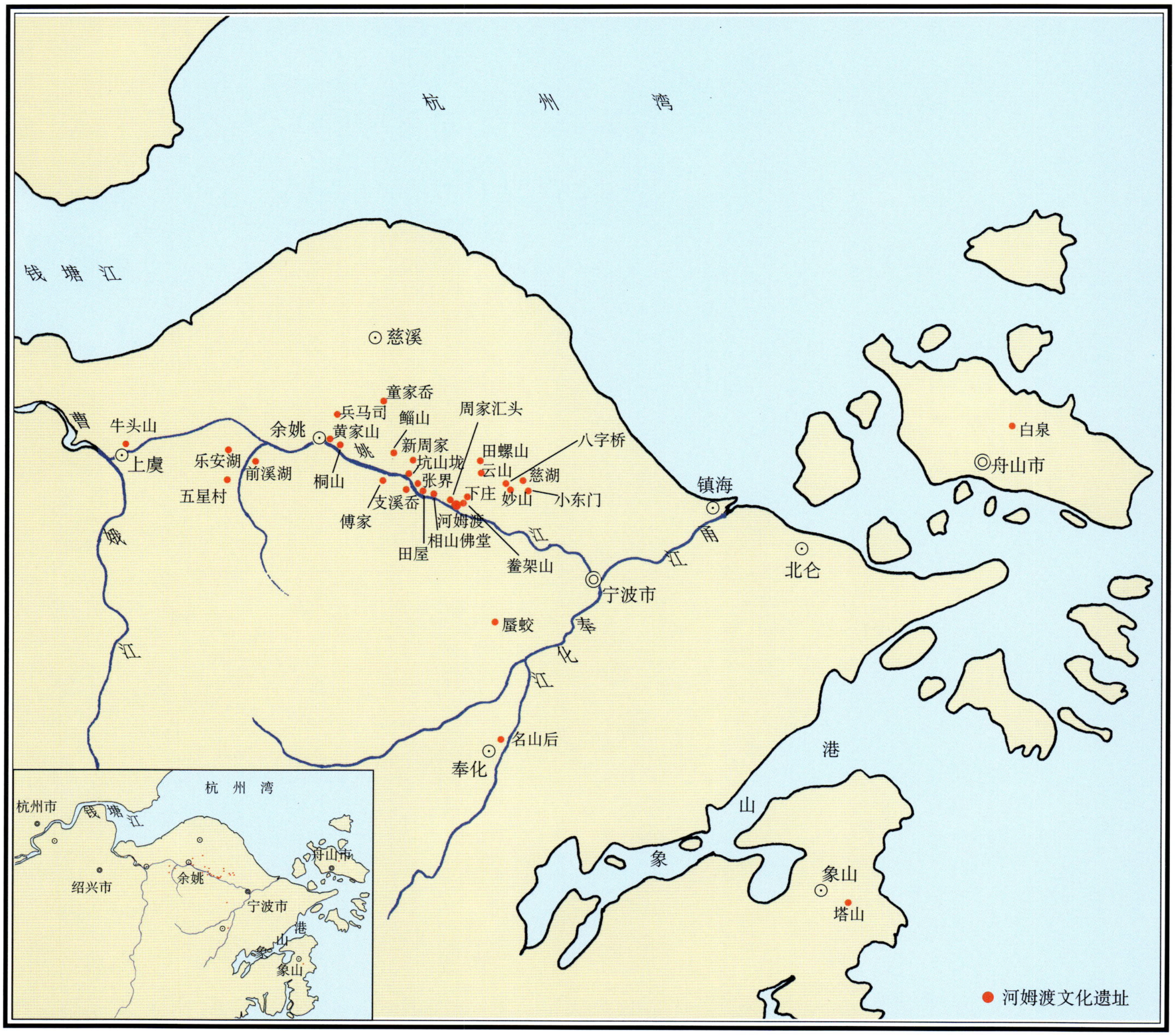

河姆渡文化遗址分布图

Layout of Hemudu culture

河姆渡文化遺跡分布図

河姆渡遗址第二次发掘现场

Second excavation spot of the Hemudu site

河姆渡遺跡第 2 次発掘現場

前　言

河姆渡遗址坐落于浙江省余姚市河姆渡镇境内。南面是碧波荡漾的姚江和重峦叠翠的四明山，沪杭甬高速公路从姚江南岸的四明山北麓通过，北面是一片宽阔的平原，萧甬铁路横穿其间。这里山青水秀，景色怡人，交通便捷，东距宁波市区 25 公里，西离余姚市区 24 公里，河姆渡旅游专线公路连接其间。

河姆渡遗址博物馆是在考古发掘的原址上兴建的史前遗址博物馆。河姆渡遗址，是 1973 年夏天当地农民兴修水利时偶然发现的。遗址总面积约 4 万平方米，文化堆积厚达 4 米左右，叠压着 4 个文化层，^{14}C 年代测定经树轮校正距今约 5000～7000 年。1973 年、1977 年先后两次发掘，揭露面积 2800 多平方米，出土石、骨、木、陶质等生产工具、生活器皿和原始艺术品等文物 6700 余件，还发现大量稻谷堆积、大面积榫卯木构建筑遗迹及丰富的动、植物遗存。河姆渡遗址的发掘为研究原始农业、家畜饲养业、建筑业、手工业和原始人的精神生活等提供了十分丰富而又弥足珍贵的实物资料。她以独特的文化面貌，被命名为“河姆渡文化”。河姆渡文化的发现表明了长江流域与黄河流域一样具有光辉灿烂的远古文化。

河姆渡遗址的发现，引起了国内外学术界的广泛关注，每年都有大批专家学者和游客慕名前来考察参观。为了有效保护和合理利用典型遗址这笔珍贵遗产，让更多的人了解 7000 年前东南沿海这颗璀璨的明珠，1993 年 5 月河姆渡遗址博物馆落成开放。博物

馆由出土文物陈列馆和遗址现场展示区两部分组成，中共中央总书记、国家主席江泽民题写了馆名。

文物陈列馆坐落在遗址的西侧，占地面积16000平方米，建筑面积3200平方米。周围绿树成荫，草地青翠，中间分布着6幢用连廊相接的建筑。建筑采用“干栏式”结构，以体现河姆渡先民的居住特征。人字形坡屋顶设置了5～7组交叉构件，再现了7000年前卓越的榫卯木作技术。整座建筑造型犹如一只展翅欲飞的大鸟，表现了河姆渡先民爱鸟、崇鸟的习俗，具有浓郁的河姆渡文化特色。

文物陈列馆有三个展厅，按概况、稻作经济、定居生活和精神文化生活等内容陈列。以河姆渡遗址出土的300多件最具代表性的文物和动植物标本为主体，辅以文字、模型、灯箱和照片等，形象生动地展示了河姆渡文化时期的生态环境以及先民的生产、生活和

河姆渡遗址博物馆
The Museum of the Hemudu Site
河姆渡遺址博物館

文物陈列展厅一角
One corner of exhibition hall of Artifact Gallery
文物陳列館の一角

精神生活等内容。

沧海桑田，斗转星移，7000年前的宁绍地区气候远比现在要温暖湿润，大致与今日广东、广西南部、海南岛和台湾的气候差不多。周围山林茂密，平原上湖泊河流遍布，沼泽发育，具有丰富多样的生态环境，为各种动、植物的生长、繁衍提供了得天独厚的适宜条件。河姆渡先民就在开发利用这些自然资源的过程中，创造了富有江南水乡特色的原始文化。

河姆渡遗址第一期文化上部大多发现了由稻谷、稻杆、稻叶和木屑等组成的稻谷堆积层，一般厚20～50厘米，最厚处超过100厘米。稻谷出土时色泽金黄新鲜，保存完好，有的连稻壳上的稃毛、隆脉及芒尖都清晰可见。经鉴定属人工栽培水稻，并已有籼、粳之分，以籼型为主。与大量稻谷伴出的170余件骨耜颇引人注目，系利用水牛等大型偶蹄

河姆渡遗址现场展示区一角
One corner of exhibition area of the Hemudu site spot
河姆渡遺跡現場展示区の一角

河姆渡渡口雕塑
Statue of Hemudu ferry
河姆渡渡し場の彫刻

类动物肩胛骨加工而成，基本保持了原骨的自然形状，是河姆渡稻作农业已进入到“耜耕农业”阶段的重要物证。另外，遗址中还发现了与稻作农业有关的中耕农具木铲、收获工具骨镰以及稻谷脱壳工具木杵等。河姆渡遗址稻谷的发现不仅纠正了我国新石器时代“有粳无籼”的说法，还证明了中国是世界上最早栽培水稻的地区之一，特别是混杂在稻谷层中的野生稻的发现，为长江下游是中国稻作农业起源地之一的观点提供了有力的证据。尽管以后又陆续发现了湖南澧县彭头山、江西万年仙人洞等比河姆渡遗址年代更早的稻作农业遗存，“但就遗址的内涵而言，都不及河姆渡那儿丰富多样，使得河姆渡迄今为止仍属中国乃至亚洲最丰富的稻作遗址”。（游修龄、郑云飞《河姆渡稻谷研究进展及展望》，《河姆渡文化研究》，杭州大学出版社，1998年）要深入、广泛开展古代稻作农业研究仍需从河姆渡遗址入手。因此，近30年来，“河姆渡”几乎成了中国稻作农业的代名词。

稻作农业的发展，为原始家畜饲养业提供了条件。河姆渡先民饲养的家畜有猪、狗、水牛三种，主要是为了满足肉食需要。由于生产力和各种自然因素的制约，当时的稻作农业和家畜饲养业仍难以满足人们的最低生活水平需要，采集和渔猎仍然是先民经济生活中不可或缺的重要组成部分。遗址中整坑成堆的橡子、芡实、菱角等植物果实和随处可见的食用后废弃的动物骨骸即是明证。

河姆渡先民房屋是以一排排桩木为基础，上面架设大、小梁承托地板，再立柱盖顶的“干栏式”建筑。“干栏式”建筑是河姆渡先民适应江南水乡环境的创造发明，这种既可以防潮又能防止野兽伤害的建筑形式，曾广泛地流行于古代南方地区。时至今日，在我国

鲻山遗址发掘现场
Excavation spot of the Zishan site
鲻山遺跡発掘現場

西南少数民族地区，依然可以见到这种古老建筑形式。河姆渡出土的木构件除大量木桩、木板和圆木外，还有上百件带榫卯的构件，表明在一些垂直相交木构节点上已采用榫卯工艺，从而把我国使用榫卯技术的历史提前到7000多年前，对中国后世传统的榫卯木构建筑产生了深远的影响，堪称为建筑史上的奇迹。

纺织技术起源于原始的编结工艺。河姆渡遗址第一、二期的木构建筑周围和一些灰坑底部发现了百余件苇席残片，小者如手掌，大者1平方米左右，编织方法科学，有垂直的斜纹和人字纹两种。绳索也发现数段，粗者如手指，由三股植物纤维搓成；细者如铁丝，由二股纤维搓成，外观与今日合掌搓成的绳子基本一致。虽然尚未发现纺织品实物，但编织纹装饰的器物却时有发现，更为重要的是发现了许多与纺织有关的工具，品种繁多而齐全，主要有纺纱工具纺轮，织布工具梭、机刀、卷布棍及缝纫工具骨针等。

舟楫的发明，反映了人类对自然环境的适应。河姆渡遗址出土的8支木桨，用整块硬木加工而成，外形同现在江南水乡农村小船上的木桨基本相近。有桨必有船，可以推测河姆渡先民已经有了用船桨作为推进工具的独木舟之类的交通工具。河姆渡遗址出土的动物遗存以水生动物为多见，特别是真鲨、鲸、灰裸顶鲷和海龟等海洋生物的发现，表明先民已凭借原始舟楫把活动范围扩大到江湖河口及近海区域。舟楫的利用既有利于获取生活资料，又扩大了对外交往的空间，为河姆渡文化晚期人们定居舟山群岛提供了可能。河姆渡文化与马家浜文化的逐渐趋同及山东长岛沿海发现相当于河姆渡文化第四期陶釜，更证明了舟楫在原始人群交往中的重要作用。

鲞架山遗址全景
Panorama of the Xiangjiashan site
鯗架山遺跡全景

河姆渡第三期文化发现的一口木构水井，由200余根桩木、长圆木等组成，分内外两部分，井底距当时地表1.35米，是我国迄今为止最早的木构水井实例。

陶器是最能代表和反映考古学文化特征的标志物之一。河姆渡文化陶器的最重要特色之一是自始至终都有夹炭陶器的存在，典型器形有拍印绳纹的陶釜和与它配合使用的支架以及鸟形盉、双耳罐、盘、豆等，器形演化规律明确，具有分期意义。根据对陶器的研究，河姆渡遗址的四个文化层，基本上代表了河姆渡文化发展的四个时期。

河姆渡先民在注重物质财富创造的同时，也注重精神文化生活的追求，着重体现在人体装饰品和原始艺术品的创作上。人体装饰品有玉石制作的玦、璜、管、珠，骨珠、笄及角、牙饰件等。原始艺术品绝大多数以装饰艺术的形式出现，既美观又实用，表现手法有刻划、戳印、浮雕、捏塑和髹漆等，题材广泛，可概括成各种短线、斜线、弦纹、波浪纹、圆圈纹等组合成的几何纹，动、植物纹和太阳纹。其中尤以反映现实生活和宗教信仰的原始艺术品最为引人瞩目，如猪纹方钵、鱼藻纹盆、稻穗纹盆、五叶纹陶块等，刻划形象生动、情趣盎然。还有猪和羊形陶塑、圆雕木鱼等，表现了河姆渡先民祈求农业和渔猎丰收、家畜兴旺的美好愿望。而用珍贵的象牙制作的圆雕鸟形象牙匕和双鸟朝阳纹、太阳纹象牙蝶形器，则反映了先民对鸟和太阳的崇拜，是原始宗教信仰的物证。

河姆渡遗址发现了20多座零星墓葬，而没有发现公共墓地。从保存较好的成年男女骨骼鉴定分析，他们的形体特征已接近于现代人，具有蒙古人种和现代澳大利亚—尼格罗人种的双重特征。

名山后遗址全景
Panorama of the Mingshanhou site
名山後遺跡全景

与其他考古学文化一样，河姆渡文化除河姆渡遗址以外，在杭州湾南岸的宁绍平原萧甬铁路两侧、宁奉平原、象山港沿岸及舟山群岛等地，已发现河姆渡文化不同时期遗存三四十处。其中经试掘和发掘的有宁波慈湖、小东门，余姚鲻山、鲞架山，奉化名山后，象山塔山等。上述材料，极大地丰富了河姆渡遗址文化内涵，填补了河姆渡文化发展中的若干缺环。

河姆渡遗址以其丰富而鲜明的文化内涵，众多的珍贵出土文物确立了其在中华民族远古文化发展史、中国考古史上的重要地位。1982年河姆渡遗址被国务院公布为全国重点文物保护单位。2001年被《考古》杂志评选为"中国20世纪百项考古大发现"之一。

遗址现场展示区位于出土文物陈列馆的东南100米的遗址范围内，紧挨姚江北岸的古渡口。占地23000平方米，展现了两次考古发掘的第一期文化木构建筑遗迹和复原的干栏式建筑群及原始先民生产劳作的场景。身临其境，仿佛进入7000年前河姆渡原始氏族村。

河姆渡遗址博物馆是我国南方第一座新石器时代的遗址博物馆，展示了我国古老而悠久的历史文化。自开馆以来，坚持常年开放，用中、英、日语免费为观众讲解，观众遍及72个国家和地区。先后荣获"浙江省文化系统先进集体"、"全国优秀爱国主义教育基地"、"全国百个爱国主义教育示范基地"等称号。这里是人们进行爱国主义教育和史前文化研究的场所，又是宁波市十佳景区之一，已经成为余姚、宁波乃至浙江省对外开放和文化交流的一个重要窗口。

塔山遗址全景
A full view of the Tashan site
塔山遺跡全景

Introduction

The Hemudu Site is situated at Hemudu township, Yuyao city, Zhejiang province. The blue Yaojiang River and green Siming Mountain lie to its south and a vast plain to its north. This is picturesque scenery with green hills, clear water and convenient communication. It is 25 kilometers east of Ningbo city proper and 24 kilometers west of Yuyao city proper, which is connected by the Hemudu tourism line.

The Museum of the Hemudu Site is a prehistoric site museum built in the original archaeological site. The Hemudu site, discovered accidentally by local villagers who built water project in summer of 1973, covers an area of 40,000 square meters with 4-meter-thick cultural deposit and 4 superimposed layers. The carbon-14 dating after tree-ring correction is 5,000-7,000 BP. The site was excavated two times in 1973 and 1977 respectively with the exposure area reaching 2,800 square meters. The excavations brought to light about 6,700 artifacts including production tools, daily utensils and primitive art works made of stone, bone, wood and pottery. In addition, they also recovered a large amount of rice remains, vast area of wooden building structure applied with tenon and mortise joints and abundant of animal and plant remains. The excavation of the Hemudu site furnishes abundant and valuable material information for research into primitive agriculture, livestock husbandry, architecture, handicraft and spiritual life of primitive inhabitants. It is named as "the Hemudu culture" in view of its distinct cultural feature. The discovery of the Hemudu culture indicates that the Yangtze River valley, the same as the Yellow River valley, has splendid culture in ancient time.

The discovery of the Hemudu site arouses wide attention in the academic circles at home and abroad, large member of experts, scholars and tourists come to examine and visit the site. In order to effectively preserve and reasonably take advantage of valuable heritage like this type site and let more people understand this prehistoric bright pearl in southeastern coastal area in 7,000 BP, the Museum of the Hemudu Site was established and opened to public in 1993. The Museum includes two parts: artifact gallery and site exhibition area. The name of the Museum is autographed by General Secretary of the Central Committee of the CPC, Chinese President Jiang Zemin.

The artifact gallery is located in the west side of the site, covers an area of 16,000 square meters with the structure area reaching 3,200 square meters. 6 buildings connected by winding corridors are distributed in the central, which are surrounded by shady trees and green meadows. The building is of pile dwelling in structure, and reflects the living characteristic of the Hemudu ancestors. The gable roof consists of 5-7 groups of intersected components, which is a picture of excellent technique of wooden tenon and mortise joints in 7,000 BP. The whole building complex is like a bird getting ready for flight, which shows the tradition that the Hemudu ancestors' love and worship for bird and has strong distinction of the Hemudu culture.

The artifact gallery consists of three exhibit halls that are arranged in order of general survey, rice economy, settled life and spiritual life. Over 300 type artifacts and animal and plant samples excavated from the Hemudu site, complement with written explanations, models, light boxes and photos, and vividly narrate the eco-environment of the Hemudu culture and production, life activity and spiritual life of ancestors.

Time brings great changes to the world and the environment changed greatly. The temperature of the Ningbo-Shaoxing area was far warmer and damper in 7,000 BP than the present, corresponded to that of today's Guangdong, southern Guangxi and that of Hainan Island and Taiwan Island. At that time, this area was surrounded by dense forest, had a vast expanse of water with lakes and lagoons well developed which provided a good and favorable condition for the growth and production of various animals and plants at the Hemudu site. In the process of exploiting the inexhaustible natural resources, the Hemudu inhabitants created the primitive culture featured with water town of Southern China.

In the upper layers of stage 1 of the Hemudu site, the organic deposit such as rice grains, stalks, leaves and wooden chips were found generally 20-50 cm thick, and even over 100 cm at the thickest place. When the rice grains were excavated, they were preserved in good condition, fresh in color, even the hair and awn of glumes could be seen clearly. Under test, the rich grains have been determined to be domesticated rice (O. Sativa) of two varieties: *indica* and *japonica* with *indica* as the dominant race. Over 170 bone spades co-existed with the rice remains were eye-catching. They are made of the scapula of artiodactyl mammals, retaining their natural form. The bone spades are crucial material evidences to prove that the rice agriculture at the Hemudu site has entered into spade tillage agriculture. Besides the tools used to turn up soil, there are also some other tools for rice cultivation, such as wooden shovels for intertillage, bone sickles for harvesting and wooden pestles used to process rice. The discovery of cultivated rice at the Hemudu site not only correct the hypothesis that "there has japonica rice, yet no indica rice in Neolithic China," but also prove that China becomes one of the earliest original regions to cultivated rice. The discovery of wild rice remains existed in the cultivated rice layers in particular, provides strong evidence to support the theory that the middle and lower Yangtze River valley is one of the original region in China to cultivated rice. Despite the earlier cultivated rice remains were found at Pengtoushan site, Lixian county, Hunan province and Xianrendong site, Wannian county, Jiangxi province in the following years, "they are not as abundant and various as in the Hemudu site in view of connotion. Therefore, the Hemudu site is still the richest cultivated rice site in China and even in Asia." (You Xiuling, Zheng Yunfei, 1998. "Progress and Prospect of the Hemudu Rice Studies" in *Studies of the Hemudu Culture*. Hangzhou: Hangzhou University Press) Provided we want to deepen and broaden the research into ancient rice agriculture, the Hemudu site is still an inevitable starting point. Consequently, "Hemudu" is almost a synonym for Chinese rice agriculture in the latest 30 years.

The agricultural development promoted animal husbandry. In order to meet meat-consumption, the Hemudu ancestors began to raise pigs, dogs and water buffaloes. However, they still remained primitive in production, which was restricted by the various natural elements so as to unable to meet the lowest living needs even though agriculture was considerably developed. Therefore, gathering, fishing and hunting still remained a subsidiary means to enlarge their food supply. Many ash-pits of wild nuts and fruits such as acorns, Gorgon fruits and water chestnuts and the scattered animal bones which being served as food and then thrown away all over the site are witnesses.

The house of Hemudu inhabitant is pile-dwelling with piles as girders to support the floor, on the floor were set columns and beams to support roof and walls. To fit the natural condition of Southern China, the Hemudu ancestors created the pile-dwelling. It had been made to prevent humidity and attacks from wild beasts, and was widely popular in ancient Southern China. To present, this ancient architecture is still existed in minority people populated area in southwest China. Besides a large amount of base boards, columns and piles, about 100 building components with tenon and mortise joints are recovered from the Hemudu site, which showed that the tenon and mortise joints method was emerged. The time when the joint-applied structure appeared in China is pushed further back to 7,000 BP. The tenon and mortise joint-applied method exerted a deep influence to wooden-structures in China and became a miracle in the history of architecture.

Weaving technology is originated from the primitive weaving and spinning craft. More than 100 fragments of reed mat were retrieved around the wooden pile-dwellings and at the bottom of ash-pits in stages 1 and 2. The small one is as palm and the big one is one square meter. The weaving methods are scientific, including twill and chevron patterns. In addition, several fragments of rope the same as the modern rope twirled by hands were found. The thick rope is as the finger twirled in three strands of plant fiber, while the thin one as wire, twirled in two strands. Though the textile material has not been found, some artifacts decorated with woven designs were retrieved occasionally. It is more important that the spinning components related to textile were discovered. Those spinning tools with great variety mainly include spinning whorls, weaving shuttles, slat battens, rollers and bone needles for sawing.

The appearance of boat is a reflection of adaptation of human being to natural environment. Eight wooden oars were excavated at the Hemudu site, which are made of a whole piece of hard wood. Their appearances are almost identical with the modern ones used in small boats in Southern China. From the oars, we can conclude that the Hemudu inhabitants might have used boat as communication tool. Aquatic animals dominate the animal remains of the Hemudu site. The discovery of sea animals such as *Carcharhinus sp.*, *Cetacea indet.*, *Gymnocraninus griseus* and *Chelonia mydas* indicate that the Hemudu ancestors' activity territory have been broadened to river tributary and offshore by boat. The invention of boat is favorable for obtaining subsistence, enlarges the spatial scope of communication and makes it possible for the Hemudu people inhabit in Zhoushan Island in the late Hemudu culture. The similarity of the Hemudu culture with the Majiabang culture and the pottery *fu*-cauldron matched with that of stage 4 of the Hemudu culture discovered in the Changdao Island, Shandong province prove that boat plays an important role in primitive communications.

One wooden structured well was found in stage 3 of the Hemudu culture. The well consists of over 200 wooden components such as columns and base boards and is divided into inner and outer parts. The bottom is 1.35 meters beneath the then surface. To present, this well is the earliest wooden structure well ever found in China.

Pottery is one of benchmarks to represent and reflect characteristics of archaeological culture. Carbon tempered pottery existed from start to end is one crucial feature of the Hemudu pottery wares. The type vessels include *fu*-cauldrons with cord mark pattern and matched supports, bird-shaped *he*-vessels, *guan*-pots with two handles, *pan*-plates and *dou*-stemmed bowls. Their evolutionary sequence is clear and can be divided into stages. According to the pottery analysis, the four layers of the Hemudu site correspond roughly to the four developmental stages of the Hemudu culture.

While created material wealth, the Hemudu ancestors are pursuing the spiritual life, the body ornaments and primitive fine art are the reflection. The body ornaments consist of jade *jue*-earrings, *huang*-pendants, tubes and beads and bone beads, bone hairpins and ivory ornaments . The primitive fine art is in the form of decorative art, which is beautiful and practical. The techniques include carving, punctuating, relief, kneading sculpture and painting. The decorative pattern can be generalized as geometric designs combined by various short lines, oblique lines, bowstring, wave and circles, animal and plant designs and sun pattern. The primitive art works reflected real life and religious belief are particularly eye-catching, such as square *bo*-bowl with pig pattern, *bo*-bowl with fish and algae, *pen*-basin with rice pattern, potsherd with five-leaf pattern, are vivid and interesting. Furthermore, pottery figurines of pig, goat and wooden fish are good wishes of pray for bump harvest of agriculture, fishing and hunting and prosperity of animal husbandry. The valuable ivory-sculpted bird-shaped daggers and ivory-sculpted butterfly-shaped ornaments with two-bird-facing-the-sun design and sun design demonstrate the Hemudu ancestors worshipped bird and sun and are regarded as the material witness of primitive religion.

Over 20 scattered tombs were found at the Hemudu site, the public cemetery has not yet been spotted. The analysis result of adult male and female skeletons show their physical characteristics are similar with modern man and have the characteristics of both Mongoloid and modern Australian-Negro race.

Like other archaeological cultures, besides the Hemudu site, several dozens of sites corresponded to different stages of the Hemudu culture have been reported. They are distributed in both sides of Xiaoshan-Ningbo Railway in the Ningbo-Shaoxing Plain, on the southern bank of the Hangzhou Bay, the Ningbo-Fenghua Plain, along Xiangshan port and the Zhoushan Islands. Among them, trial excavations and excavations have been carried out in Cihu and Xiao Dongmen of Ningbo, Zishan and Xiangjiashan of Yuyao, Mingshanhou of Fenghua, Tashan of Xiangshan, Loujiaqiao of Zhuji. The above mentioned information greatly richens the cultural contents of the Hemudu site and fills several missing links of the

Hemudu culture in the developmental process.

Owing to its richest and distinctive cultural connotation and abundant valuable artifacts, the Hemudu site plays an important role in the developmental history of ancient Chinese culture and in the history of Chinese archaeology. In 1982, the Hemudu site was proclaimed as "Major Historical Monuments and Cultural Relics under State Protection." In 2001, the Hemudu site was selected as one of "100 Major Archaeological Discoveries in the 20th Century in China" which was sponsored by Archaeology Publications.

The site museum lies in 100 meters southeast of the artifact gallery and is adjacent closely to the ancient ferry on the north bank of the Yaojiang River. It covers an area of 23,000 square meters and exhibits wooden building structure remains, reconstruction of pile-dwelling complex and working scene of primitive ancestors of the Hemudu culture stage 1. The scene is so vividly portrayed that the reader feels as if he is entering the Hemudu primitive village in 7,000 BP.

The Museum of the Hemudu Site is the first Neolithic site museum in South China, which reveals the long-lasting historical culture of ancient China. Since its opening to public, the Museum adheres to open all year round and to provide free guide in Chinese, English and Japanese languages. The visitors extend all over 72 countries and regions. The Museum is also awarded as "Advanced Collective of Zhejiang Provincial Cultural System," "National Excellent Patriotism Education Base" and one of "100 Patriotism Education Exemplary Bases in China." This is the place for patriotism education and studies of prehistoric culture, as well as one of ten best scenic spots of Ningbo City. The Museum becomes an important window for opening to Western countries and cultural exchanges in Yuyao, Ningbo and even in Zhejiang province.

前　言

河姆渡遺跡は浙江省余姚市河姆渡鎮境内にある。南は青い波が揺らめく姚江と緑の山々が連なる四明山で、滬杭甬高速道路が姚江南岸の四明山北麓から通じ、北面は広い平原で、蕭甬鉄道がその間を横断している。ここは山紫水明で景色がよく、交通の便もよい。東へ寧波市区まで25km、西は余姚市区から24km離れている。河姆渡旅遊専線公路がその間を結んでいる。

河姆渡遺址博物館は発掘区に建てられた先史時代の遺跡博物館である。遺跡は1973年夏、水利工事の際に当地の農民が偶然発見した。総面積は約40000m^2で、文化層の堆積は4m前後に達し、4つの文化層が重なり合っている。^{14}C年代測定値を年輪年代により補正した結果、その時期は約5000～7000年前である。1973年と1977年に前後2回の調査が行われ、2800m^2を発掘し、石、骨、木、土などの材料で製作された生産工具や工芸品などの遺物が6700点余り出土した。さらに大量の稲籾の堆積、大面積の木組みによる木造建築遺構と豊富な動植物遺存体が発見された。河姆渡遺跡の発掘により、初期農耕、家畜の飼育、建築、手工業や古代人の芸術・信仰等の研究に関する多くの貴重な実物資料が得られた。そしてその文化の特徴的な内容から「河姆渡文化」と命名された。河姆渡文化の発見は、長江流域にも黄河流域と同様に輝ける古代文化が存在したことを証明したのである。

河姆渡遺跡の発見は国内外の学術界から注目され、毎年多くの専門家や旅行者がその名を慕い、視察や見学に訪れた。この貴重な遺産の効果的な保護とモデル遺跡としての合理的な利用のため、またより多くの人々が7000年前の東南沿海部の輝ける先史時代の珠玉を理解できるよう、1993年5月に河姆渡遺址博物館は落成し公開された。出土文物陳列館と遺址現場展示区の2館に分けて作られ、中国共産党中央総書記、国家主席である江沢民が館名の題字を記した。

文物陳列館は遺跡の西側に位置し、16000m^2ほどを占め、建物の規模は3200m^2である。周囲は木が茂り、芝生は緑豊かで、その中には六棟の廊下によって結ばれた建物がある。それは「高床式」結構を採用し、河姆渡先住民の居住形態の特徴を表している。切妻造りの屋根の頂上には交差した木材を5～7組設置し、7000年前の優れた木組みの技術を再現している。建物の全体の造型は大きく翼をのばして羽ばたく鳥のようであり、河姆渡先住民の愛鳥・崇鳥習俗を表現しており、河姆渡文化の強い特色を備えている。

文物陳列館は3つの展示室があり、概観、稲作経済、定住生活と芸術・信仰などの内容を展示している。河姆渡遺跡から出土した300点余りの最も代表的な遺物と動植物標本を主体とし、文章、模型、ライトボックスと写真などで補足し、生き生きとしたイメージで河姆渡文化時期の生態環境と先住民の生業、生活、芸術・信仰などの展示を行っている。

滄海変じて桑畑となり、光陰矢のごときであり、7000年前の寧紹地区の気候は現在に比べてやや温暖湿潤で、およそ現在の広東、広西南部、海南島や台湾の気候と似ていた。周囲には森林が生い茂り、平原には湖や河川があまねく分布し、沼沢が発達しており、多種多様な生態環境であった。そのため各種の動植物の成長と繁殖に非常に適した条件を備えていた。河姆渡先住民はこれらの自然資源を開発し利用していく過程で、江南水郷の特徴的な先史文化を創り上げていったのである。

河姆渡遺跡第1期文化層の上部では、大部分に稲の籾、茎、葉と木屑などが混ざった稲の堆積層が発見され、一般に厚さは20～50cm、最も厚いところで100cmを越える。籾は出土時には鮮やかな黄金色に輝いており、保存は完全で、ある籾殻の上には稃毛、隆脈と芒がはっきりと残っていた。鑑定によるとこれらは人工栽培水稲で、さらに「籼」稲(細長いタイプ)と「粳」稲(丸いタイプ)に分かれており、「籼」稲が主であった。大量の稲籾に伴って出土した170点余りの骨耜(鋤)は非常に注目される。これらは水牛等の大型偶蹄類動物の肩胛骨を加工して作られており、基本的に本来の骨の形状を保っている。これは、河姆渡の稲作農耕がすでに「耜耕農業」の段階にあったことの重要な証拠である。このほかに、稲作農耕と関係のある中耕農具の木鏟、収穫工具の骨鎌および脱穀工具の木杵などが遺跡中で発見された。河姆渡遺跡の稲籾の発見により、新石器時代の「有粳無籼」の説が修正されただけでなく、さらに中国が世界でも最古の水稲栽培地区の一つであることを証明した。特に稲籾層に混じって発見された野生稲は、長江下流域が中国における稲作農耕の起源地の一つであるという説の有力な証拠となった。以後続々と湖南省澧県彭頭山、江西省万年県仙人洞など、河姆渡遺跡に比べてさらに早い時期の稲作農耕に関する遺跡が発見されたが、「遺跡の内容は河姆渡ほどの豊富な多様さには及ばず、これまでのところ河姆渡は依然として中国あるいはアジアで最も内容豊かな稲作遺跡となっている。(游修齢、鄭雲飛「河姆渡稲谷研究進展及展望」『河姆渡文化研究』杭州大学出版社、1998年10月)広範な古代稲作農耕の研究を行うには依然として河姆渡遺跡から取りかかる必要がある。よってこの30年間で「河姆渡」は中国稲作農耕の代名詞となったと言える。

稲作農耕の発展は家畜飼育の条件を整える。河姆渡先住民の飼育した家畜は豚、犬、水牛の3種類であり、主に食肉としてであった。生産力と各種の自然条件の制約により、当時の稲作農耕と家畜の飼育は最低水準の需要を満たすものではなく、採集・狩猟・漁撈は彼らの生業の中で欠かすことのできない重要な部分であった。遺跡中のゴミ穴の中から多くのドングリ、オニバス、ヒシの実などの植物遺存体が出土し、食用廃棄物である動物骨が随所で見られることなどがこの証拠である。

河姆渡先住民の住居は杭列を基礎とし、大小の梁を架け渡して床板を張り、さらに柱を載せて屋根を作る「高床式」建築である。「高床式」建築は河姆渡先住民が江南水郷の環境に合わせて発明したものであり、湿気や野獣の驚異を防ぐことのできるこの類の建築形式は古代の南方地区で流行した。現在でも、中国西南の少数民族地区では依然としてこの類の古い建築形式を見ることができる。河姆渡出土の木材は大量の木杭、木板と丸木のほかに、100点以上の枘・枘穴を持つ材木があり、これは材木を垂直に組み合わせる際に、すでに枘接ぎ技法を採用していたことを示している。中国における枘接ぎ技法の歴史は7000年前までにさかのぼり、後世の伝統的な木組みの木造建築に深い影響を与えており、これは建築史上の奇跡と言えよう。

紡織技術は原始的な編み物工芸を元にして発達する。河姆渡遺跡第1期、2期の木造建築の周囲と一部のゴミ穴の底部では100点以上のアンペラの破片が発見されている。小さいものは手のひら大で、大きいものは1m^{2}前後ある。編み方はとても優れており、垂直の斜文と人字文の2種がある。縄は数段撚りのものが発見されており、粗い縄は指のような太さで、三本の植物纖維を撚り合わせている。細い縄はハリガネのような細さで、二本の植物纖維を撚り合わせている。外観は現在の合掌撚りの縄と基本的に同じである。織物の実物はまだ未発見であるが、編文で装飾した器物はすでに発見されている。さらに重要なのは多くの紡織に関係する工具の発見で、種類も多様であり、主なものには紡織工具の紡錘車、機織り工具の梭、緯打具、布巻きと裁縫工具の骨針などがある。

舟の発明は人類の自然環境に対する適応を表している。河姆渡遺跡出土の8点の木櫂は一本の堅い木から作られ、外形は現在の江南水郷の農村で使われる小舟用の木櫂と基本的に相似している。木櫂が存在するので舟があった可能性が高く、河姆渡の先住民がすでに木櫂を使って漕ぐ独木舟の類の交通手段を持っていたことが推測できる。河姆渡遺跡出土の動物遺存体は水生動物が多く、特別なものとして鮫、鯨、メイチ鯛や海亀などの海洋生物が見つかっており、彼らがすでに原始的な舟で活動範囲を近辺の河口から近海付近へと拡大していったことを物語っている。舟の利用は生活の糧を得るのに有用で、また交流地域を拡大することになり、河姆渡文化晩期の人々が舟山群島に定住することを可能にした。河姆渡文化と馬家浜文化の融合や、山東の長島沿海における河姆渡文化第4期相当の土器釜の発見は、舟が古代人の交流に重要な役割を果たしていたことを証明している。

河姆渡第3期文化では木造の井戸が1つ発見されている。200本余りの杭と丸木を使い、内外両部分に分かれており、井戸の底は当時の地表から1.35mで、これまでに中国で発見された中で最古の木造井戸の実例である。

土器は考古学文化の特徴を最もよく反映する標識の一つである。河姆渡文化の土器の最も重要な特徴として終始夾炭陶(胎土中に植物質の混和材が混ぜられ、それが炭化して残っている土器)が存在することがあげられる。典型的な器形は縄席文を施した釜とそれに組み合わせて使う支脚、そして鳥形盉、双耳罐、盤、豆などである。器形の変化は明確であり、分期する際に有効である。土器の研究に基づくと、河姆渡遺跡の4つの文化層は基本的にそれぞれ河姆渡文化の第1～4期の各時期に相当する。

河姆渡先住民は物質的な豊かさ求めると同時に、精神的な文化の追求にも注力している。それは主として装飾品と原始芸術の創作に現れている。装飾品は玉・石製の玦、璜、管、珠および骨珠、骨笄、角牙装飾品などである。原始芸術品はほとんど器物の装飾として見られ、美しくかつ実用的で、表現手法には刻線、型押し、浮き彫り、手捏と漆塗りなどがある。文様は幅広く、各種の短線、斜線、弦文、波浪文、円圏文などを組み合わせた幾何学文、動物文、植物文と太陽文に概括できる。その中で現実生活と宗教信仰を反映した原始芸術品が最も注目され、豚文方鉢、魚藻文盆、稲穂文盆、五葉文陶塊(粘土を焼いて作った板状のもの)などは生き生きとしたイメージを刻み、情緒にあふれている。そのほか豚形土偶、羊形土偶、丸彫りの木魚などには、河姆渡先住民の農耕、狩猟、漁撈の豊かな収穫や家畜の成長への祈願が表現されている。さらに貴重な象牙を用いて製作された丸彫りの鳥形象牙匕や双鳥朝陽文、太陽文象牙蝶形器などには先住民の鳥と太陽に関する崇拝が現れており、原始的な宗教信仰の物証となっている。

河姆渡遺跡では20基あまりの墓葬がまばらに発見されているのみで、公共墓地もない。保存が比較的よい青年男女の骨の鑑定分析によると、彼らの形質的特徴は現代人に近く、モンゴロイドと現代オーストラロ-ネグロイドの両方の特徴を持っている。

その他の考古学文化と同様、河姆渡文化では河姆渡遺跡のほかに、すでに杭州湾南岸の寧紹平原蕭甬鉄道の両側、寧奉平原、象山港沿岸と舟山群島などで河姆渡文化の異なる時期に属する30～40カ所の遺跡が発見されている。その内で試掘や発掘が実施された遺跡には寧波慈湖、小東門、余姚鲻山、鶱架山、奉化名山後、象山塔山、諸暨楼家橋などがある。これらの資料により、河姆渡文化遺跡の様相がさらに豊富になり、河姆渡文化の発展における若干のミッシングリンクが補われた。

河姆渡遺跡の豊かで鮮明な内容と多くの貴重な出土遺物は、中国古代文化の発展史、中国考古学史において重要な地位を確立した。1982年、河姆渡遺跡は国務院公布により全国重点文物保護単位となった。2001年には雑誌『考古』が「中国20世紀百項考古大発現」の一つに選出した。

遺址現場展示区は、出土文物陳列館の東南100mの遺跡範囲内にあり、姚江北岸の古い渡し場に近い。23000m^{2}の中に、2度の発掘で出土した第1期文化の木造建築遺構と復元した高床式建築群および住民の生活風景を展示している。そこに身を置けば、さながら7000年前の河姆渡の古代集落にいるかのようである。

河姆渡遺址博物館は中国南方における初めての新石器時代の遺跡博物館であり、中国悠久の歴史と文化を展示している。開館以来、一年中公開し、中国語、英語、日本語で観客に対して無料の説明を行い、観客は72の国家と地区に及ぶ。また前後して「浙江省文化伝統先進集体」「全国優秀愛国主義教育基地」「全国百個愛国主義教育示範基地」などの称号を得ている。ここは愛国主義教育と先史文化研究を押し進める場所であり、寧波市の十佳境区のうちの一つである。すでに余姚、寧波、浙江省の対外開放と文化交流の重要な窓口となっている。

玉　石　器

Jade，Stone Artifacts

玉　石　器

河姆渡文化石器普遍较小，器形以斧、锛、凿等生产工具为大宗。第一、二期的石料大多是硬度高、韧性好的黑色或深灰色燧石、硅质岩等。因进行整器精细磨砺费工费时，故除刃部精磨外，其余部位尚留有打琢痕迹，甚至还有打制石器在继续使用。第三期开始，随着硬度稍低的泥质硅质岩和凝灰岩大量出现，精细磨制技术得以迅速推广，器形因此变得规整，轮廓分明，器物制作精细，管钻技术使用广泛，新出现耜、刀、纺轮等。人体装饰品主要是用萤石、石英等制作的玦、璜、管、珠等小件器物及少量闪玉装饰品。

The stone implements recovered from the Hemudu culture are small, common types are axes, adzes, and chisels. In the stages 1 and 2, the resources mainly are black or blackish gray flint and siliceous stone with high hardness and good durability. Due to need manpower and time to delicately polish the whole artifact, only the edge is polished carefully, other parts are chipped, even the chipped stone tools were still used. In the stage 3, argillaceous siliceous stone and tuff in relatively lower hardness emerged quantitatively, the polish technology spread quickly. The types of stone industry are tidy, the shapes are clear and the handcraft is delicate. The tube-perforation technology is appeared. The new types of tools consisting of hoe blade, knife and spindle whorl emerged. The objects that are artistic and decorative in nature include *jue*-earrings, *huang*-pendants, tubes and beads made of fluorite and quartz. The ornaments made of jade are few.

河姆渡文化の石器は一般に小型で、器種は斧、手斧、鑿などの生産工具が主である。第1、2期の石材は多くが硬度が高く強靭な黒色あるいは深灰色のチャート、硅質岩などである。全体を細かく研磨することに手間がかかるため、刃部を精巧に磨いているが、その他の部分には敲打痕が残っている。さらには打製石器も継続して使用されている。第3期にはやや硬度が低い泥質硅質岩や凝灰岩が大量に使われ始め、精巧な研磨技術を素早く広めることができた。ゆえに器形は規則的に変化し、輪郭が明確で製作は精緻であり、穿孔技術の使用も広まり、新しく耜、刀、紡錘車などが出現する。装飾品は主に蛍石、石英などによって製作した玦、璜、管、珠などの小型のものと少量の軟玉製の装飾品がある。

1

斧
左：T235（4A）:128
长 6.5、刃宽 4.8 厘米
右：T211（3B）:15
长 5.5、刃宽 3.8 厘米
河姆渡文化一、二期
1977 年河姆渡遗址出土
河姆渡遗址博物馆藏

AXES
Left: T235 (4A):128
L 6.5 cm　W 4.8 cm (blade)
Right: T211 (3B):15
L 5.5 cm　W 3.8 cm (blade)
Stages 1 and 2 of Hemudu culture
Unearthed from the Hemudu site in 1977
Collected in the Museum of the Hemudu Site

斧
左：T235（4A）:128
長 6.5 cm　刃部幅 4.8 cm
右：T211（3B）:15
長 5.5 cm　刃部幅 3.8 cm
河姆渡文化 1、2 期
1977 年河姆渡遺跡出土
河姆渡遺址博物館藏

2

穿孔斧

T18（1）:3

长 11.6、宽 8.8、厚 1.6 厘米

河姆渡文化四期

1973 年河姆渡遗址出土

浙江省博物馆藏

AXE

T18（1）:3

L 11.6 cm　W 8.8 cm　T 1.6 cm

Stage 4 of Hemudu culture

Unearthed from the Hemudu site in 1973

Collected in Zhejing Provincial Museum

穿孔斧

T18（1）:3

長 11.6 cm　幅 8.8 cm　厚さ1.6 cm

河姆渡文化 4 期

1973 年河姆渡遺跡出土

浙江省博物館蔵

3

锛

左：T222（2A）:19
　　长 3.4、刃宽 3.1 厘米
右：T243（2B）:10
　　长 7.2、刃宽 4.2 厘米
河姆渡文化三期
1977 年河姆渡遗址出土
河姆渡遗址博物馆藏

ADZES

Left: T222 (2A):19
　　L 3.4 cm　W 3.1 cm (blade)
Right: T243 (2B):10
　　L 7.2 cm　W 4.2 cm (blade)
Stage 3 of Hemudu culture
Unearthed from the Hemudu site in 1977
Collected in the Museum of the Hemudu Site

手斧

左：T222（2A）:19
　　長 3.4 cm　刃部幅 3.1 cm
右：T243（2B）:10
　　長 7.2 cm　刃部幅 4.2 cm
河姆渡文化 3 期
1977 年河姆渡遺跡出土
河姆渡遺址博物館藏

4

凿

左：T216（2B）:11

长 6.5、宽 2.8、厚 2.5 厘米

右：T225（2B）:12

长 7.5、宽 1.5、厚 2.5 厘米

河姆渡文化三期

1977 年河姆渡遗址出土

河姆渡遗址博物馆藏

CHISELS

Left：T216（2B）:11

L 6.5 cm　W 2.8 cm　T 2.5 cm

Right：T225（2B）:12

L 7.5 cm　W 1.5 cm　T 2.5 cm

Stage 3 of Hemudu culture

Unearthed from the Hemudu site in 1977

Collected in the Museum of the Hemudu Site

鑿

左：T216（2B）:11

長 6.5 cm　幅 2.8 cm　厚さ2.5 cm

右：T225（2B）:12

長 7.5 cm　幅 1.5 cm　厚さ2.5 cm

河姆渡文化 3 期

1977 年河姆渡遺跡出土

河姆渡遺址博物館藏

5

刀

T242（2B）:18

残长 5.1、宽 4.5、厚 0.7 厘米

河姆渡文化三期

1977 年河姆渡遗址出土

河姆渡遗址博物馆藏

CUTTER

T242（2B）:18

Surviving L 5.1 cm W 4.5 cm T 0.7 cm

Stage 3 of Hemudu culture

Unearthed from the Hemudu site in 1977

Collected in the Museum of the Hemudu Site

刀

T242（2B）:18

残長 5.1 cm 幅 4.5 cm 厚さ0.7 cm

河姆渡文化 3 期

1977 年河姆渡遺跡出土

河姆渡遺址博物館蔵

6

钻形器

T1010（7）:3

长 6.9 厘米

河姆渡文化四期

1990 年塔山遗址出土

象山县文物管理委员会藏

DRILL SHAPED TOOL

T1010（7）:3

L 6.9 cm

Stage 4 of Hemudu culture

Unearthed from the the Tashan site in 1990

Collected in the Xiangshan County CPAM

鑽形器

T1010（7）:3

長 6.9 cm

河姆渡文化 4 期

1990 年塔山遺跡出土

象山県文物管理委員会蔵

7

弹丸

左 1：T234（3B）:85
直径 1.1 厘米
左 2：T244（3B）:33
直径 1.4 厘米
中：T243（3A）:41
直径 2.0 厘米
右 2：T35（3）:24
直径 1.3 厘米
右 1：T235（3B）:75
直径 1.3 厘米
河姆渡文化二期
1973、1977 年河姆渡遗址出土
河姆渡遗址博物馆藏

PELLETS

Left 1：T234（3B）:85
D 1.1 cm
Left 2：T244（3B）:33
D 1.4 cm
Middle：T243（3A）:41
D 2.0 cm
Right 2：T35（3）:24
D 1.3 cm
Right 1：T235（3B）:75
D 1.3 cm
Stage 2 of Hemudu culture
Unearthed from the Hemudu site in 1973，1977
Collected in the Museum of the Hemudu Site

弹丸

左 1：T234（3B）:85
直径 1.1 cm
左 2：T244（3B）:33
直径 1.4 cm
中：T243（3A）:41
直径 2.0 cm
右 2：T35（3）:24
直径 1.3 cm
右 1：T235（3B）:75
直径 1.3 cm
河姆渡文化 2 期
1973、1977 年河姆渡遺跡出土
河姆渡遺址博物館藏

8

纺轮
T231（3B）:33
直径 5.9、厚 0.8 厘米
河姆渡文化二期
1977 年河姆渡遗址出土
河姆渡遗址博物馆藏

SPINDLE WHORL
T231（3B）:33
D 5.9 cm　T 0.8 cm
Stage 2 of Hemudu culture
Unearthed from the Hemudu site in 1977
Collected in the Museum of the Hemudu Site

紡錘車
T231（3B）:33
直径 5.9 cm　厚さ0.8 cm
河姆渡文化 2 期
1977 年河姆渡遺跡出土
河姆渡遺址博物館蔵

9

坠

左：T243（4A）:272

长 4.5、直径 2.8 厘米

右：T214（3B）:35

长 4.6、宽 3.9、厚 2.3 厘米

河姆渡文化一、二期

1977 年河姆渡遗址出土

河姆渡遗址博物馆藏

PENDANTS

Left：T243（4A）:272

L 4.5 cm D 2.8 cm

Right：T214（3B）:35

L 4.6 cm W 3.9 cm T 2.3 cm

Stages 1 and 2 of Hemudu culture

Unearthed from the Hemudu site in 1977

Collected in the Museum of the Hemudu Site

錘

左：T243（4A）:272

長 4.5 cm 直径 2.8 cm

右：T214（3B）:35

長 4.6 cm 幅 3.9 cm 厚さ2.3 cm

河姆渡文化 1、2 期

1977 年河姆渡遺跡出土

河姆渡遺址博物館蔵

10

砺石
T226（3A）
长 18.5、宽 19.7、厚 5.1 厘米
河姆渡文化二期
1977 年河姆渡遗址出土
河姆渡遗址博物馆藏

WHETSTONE
T226（3A）
L 18.5 cm　W 19.7 cm　T 5.1 cm
Stage 2 of Hemudu culture
Unearthed from the Hemudu site in 1977
Collected in the Museum of the Hemudu Site

砥石
T226（3A）
長 18.5 cm　幅 19.7 cm　厚さ5.1 cm
河姆渡文化 2 期
1977 年河姆渡遺跡出土
河姆渡遺址博物館蔵

11

燧石器

河姆渡文化一、二期

1996 年鲻山遗址出土

浙江省文物考石研究所藏

FLINT ARTIFACT

Stages 1 and 2 of Hemudu culture

Unearthed from the the Zishan site in 1996

Collected in Zhejiang Provincial Institute of Cultural Relics and Archaeology

燧石器

河姆渡文化 1、2 期

1996 年鯔山遺跡出土

浙江省文物考古研究所蔵

12

管形珠

左 1：T221（4A）:87

长 1.2、直径 0.9 厘米

左 2：T33（4）:65

长 1.9、直径 1.4 厘米

管

中：T244（4A）:133

长 2.5、直径 1.6 厘米

右 2：T234（4B）:299

长 3.0、直径 1.5 厘米

右 1：T1（4）:104

长 3.1、直径 2.9 厘米

河姆渡文化一期

1973、1977 年河姆渡遗址出土

浙江省博物馆藏

TUBE-SHAPED BEADS

Left 1：T221（4A）:87

L 1.2 cm D 0.9 cm

Left 2：T33（4）:65

L 1.9 cm D 1.4 cm

TUBES

Middle：T244（4A）:133

L 2.5 cm D 1.6 cm

Right 2：T234（4B）:299

L 3.0 cm D 1.5 cm

Right 1：T1（4）:104

L 3.1 cm D 2.9 cm

Stage 1 of Hemudu culture

Unearthed from the Hemudu site in 1973，1977

Collected in Zhejiang Provincial Museum

管形珠

左 1：T221（4A）:87

長 1.2 cm 直径 0.9 cm

左 2：T33（4）:65

長 1.9 cm 直径 1.4 cm

管

中：T244（4A）:133

長 2.5 cm 直径 1.6 cm

右 2：T234（4B）:299

長 3.0 cm 直径 1.5 cm

右 1：T1（4）:104

長 3.1 cm 直径 2.9 cm

河姆渡文化 1 期

1973、1977 年河姆渡遺跡出土

浙江省博物館蔵

13

玦

T2:6

外径 4.6、内径 2.3、厚 0.8 厘米

1973 年河姆渡遗址出土

浙江省博物馆藏

***JUE* – EARRING**

T2:6

D 4.6 cm (outer) D 2.3 cm (inner) T 0.8 cm

Unearthed from the Hemudu site in 1973

Collected in Zhejiang Provincial Museum

玦

T2:6

外径 4.6 cm 内径 2.3 cm 厚さ0.8 cm

1973 年河姆渡遺跡出土

浙江省博物館蔵

14

玉玦

左：M17:2

外径 4.0、内径 1.8 厘米

右：M10:2

外径 4.6、内径 2.3 厘米

河姆渡文化三期

1990 年塔山遗址出土

浙江省文物考古研究所、

象山县文物管理委员会藏

JADE *JUE* – EARRINGS

Left：M17:2

D 4.0 cm（outer） D 1.8 cm（inner）

Right：M10:2

D 4.6 cm（outer） D 2.3 cm（inner）

Stage 3 of Hemudu culture

Unearthed from the Tashan site in 1990

Collected in Zhejiang Provincial Institute of Cultural Relics and Archaeology and the Xiangshan County CPAM respectively

玉玦

左：M17:2

外徑 4.0 cm 内徑 1.8 cm

右：M10:2

外徑 4.6 cm 内徑 2.3 cm

河姆渡文化 3 期

1990 年塔山遺跡出土

浙江省文物考古研究所、

象山県文物管理委員会藏

15

璜
T244（4B）:299
长 4.4 厘米
河姆渡文化一期
1977 年河姆渡遗址出土
浙江省博物馆藏

***HUANG* - PENDANT**
T244（4B）:299
L 4.4 cm
Stage 1 of Hemudu culture
Unearthed from the Hemudu site in 1977
Collected in Zhejiang Provincial Museum

璜
T224（4B）:299
長 4.4 cm
河姆渡文化 1 期
1977 年河姆渡遺跡出土
浙江省博物館藏

16

蝶形器

T28（4）:41

长 11.3、宽 8.0 厘米

河姆渡文化一期

1973 年河姆渡遗址出土

浙江省博物馆藏

BUTTERFLY-SHAPED ORNAMENT

T28（4）:41

L 11.3 cm　W 8.0 cm

Stage 1 of Hemudu culture

Unearthed from the Hemudu site in 1977

Collected in Zhejiang Provincial Museum

蝶形器

T28（4）:41

長 11.3 cm　幅 8.0 cm

河姆渡文化 1 期

1973 年河姆渡遺跡出土

浙江省博物館藏

骨、角、牙器

Bone，Antler，Ivory，Tooth Artifacts

骨、角、牙器

大量使用骨（角、牙）器是河姆渡文化的显著特征之一，主要用于农业生产、狩猎捕捞、纺织缝纫以及装饰艺术中。器形有耜、镞、哨、针、凿、锥、管状针、刀、匕、鱼镖、笄、蝶形器和骨、牙、角饰件等近20种。数量众多的骨器大都发现于河姆渡文化一、二期，之后数量和种类迅速减少。在制作方法上，尽量利用动物的各种骨、角、牙的自然形态，稍作简单的错磨加工；也有一部分系利用剖开的动物管状骨，加工工艺比较复杂。而少量以象牙等珍贵材料加工的原始艺术品，则灵活地运用了圆雕、透雕及阴线刻划等艺术手法。鸟成为艺术表现的主题。

The application of the most numerous bone (antler, ivory) implements is one of outstanding features of the Hemudu culture. They mainly used in agricultural production, hunting and fishing, textile and sawing industry and decorative art. The types include hoe blades, arrowheads, whistles, needles, chisels, awls, tube-shaped needles, spatulas, knives, air bladders of fish, hairpins, butterfly-shaped tools, and ornaments, altogether is about 20 kinds. The large amount of bone implements were greatly recovered from stages 1 and 2 of the Hemudu culture, they were decreased sharply in quantity and types afterward. In view of making craft, objects are making of the natural material and polished briefly. Only a small part of bones are split and applied complex technology. The very rare primitive art works made of ivory are decorated with sculpture, openwork and intaglio designs. The bird is the major motif in decoration.

大量に骨（角、牙）器を使用するのは河姆渡文化の顕著な特徴の一つである。これらは主に農耕、狩猟、漁撈、紡織および装飾品に使われる。器種は耜、鏃、哨、針、鑿、錐、管状針、刀、匕、銛、笄、蝶形器と骨、牙、角製飾りなど20種近い。大量の骨器はほとんどが河姆渡文化第1、2期に見られ、のちに数量、種類とも急速に減少する。製作技術を見ると、ほとんどが動物の各種骨、牙、角の自然形態をそのまま利用し、やや簡単な研磨加工を施している。動物の割った管状骨を利用したものもあり、加工技術は比較的複雑である。少量の象牙などの貴重な原料を加工した原始芸術品には丸彫り、透かし彫りや陰線刻などの技法を活用している。鳥が芸術表現の主題となっている。

17

耜

T211（4A）:219

残长 22.0、刃宽 15.3、厚 0.9 厘米

河姆渡文化一期

1977 年河姆渡遗址出土

河姆渡遗址博物馆藏

***SI* – SPADE**

T211（4A）:219

Surviving L 22.0 cm　W 15.3 cm（blade）　T 0.9 cm

Stage 1 of Hemudu culture

Unearthed from the Hemudu site in 1977

Collected in the Museum of the Hemudu Site

耜

T211（4A）:219

残長 22.0 cm　刃部幅 15.3 cm　厚さ0.9 cm

河姆渡文化 1 期

1977 年河姆渡遺跡出土

河姆渡遺址博物館蔵

18
耜
T211（4B）:381
长 22.0、刃宽 13.0、厚 3.4 厘米
河姆渡文化一期
1977 年河姆渡遗址出土
河姆渡遗址博物馆藏

SI **– SPADE**
T211（4B）:381
L 22.0 cm　W 13.0 cm（blade）　T 3.4 cm
Stage 1 of Hemudu culture
Unearthed from the Hemudu site in 1977
Collected in the Museum of the Hemudu Site

耜
T211（4B）:381
長 22.0 cm　刃部幅 13.0 cm　厚さ3.4 cm
河姆渡文化 1 期
1977 年河姆渡遺跡出土
河姆渡遺址博物館蔵

19
耜
T211（4B）:468
长 16.5、刃宽 8.6、厚 3.7 厘米
河姆渡文化一期
1977 年河姆渡遗址出土
河姆渡遗址博物馆藏

SI **– SPADE**
T211（4B）:468
L 16.5 cm　W 8.6 cm（blade）　T 3.7 cm
Stage 1 of Hemudu culture
Unearthed from the Hemudu site in 1977
Collected in the Museum of the Hemudu Site

耜
T211（4B）:468
長 16.5 cm　刃部幅 8.6 cm　厚さ3.7 cm
河姆渡文化 1 期
1977 年河姆渡遺跡出土
河姆渡遺址博物館蔵

20

绑柄耜

T224（4B）:175

长 18.0、刃宽 9.8 厘米

河姆渡文化一期

1977 年河姆渡遗址出土

浙江省博物馆藏

***SI* – SPADE WITH SHAFT**

T224（4B）:175

L 18.0 cm　W 9.8 cm（blade）

Stage 1 of Hemudu culture

Unearthed from the Hemudu site in 1977

Collected in Zhejiang Provincial Museum

柄の残る耜

T224（4B）:175

長 18.0 cm　刃部幅 9.8 cm

河姆渡文化 1 期

1977 年河姆渡遺跡出土

浙江省博物館蔵

21

耜

T211（4B）:491

长 27.4、厚 1.9 厘米

河姆渡文化一期

1977 年河姆渡遗址出土

河姆渡遗址博物馆藏

SI – SPADE

T211（4B）:491

L 27.4 cm　T 1.9 cm

Stage 1 of Hemudu culture

Unearthed from the Hemudu site in 1977

Collected in the Museum of the Hemudu Site

耜

T211（4B）:491

長 27.4 cm　厚さ1.9 cm

河姆渡文化 1 期

1977 年河姆渡遺跡出土

河姆渡遺址博物館蔵

22

镰形器

T214（4A）:97

残长 17.5、宽 3.0 厘米

河姆渡文化一期

1977 年河姆渡遗址出土

浙江省博物馆藏

SICKLE-SHAPED TOOL

T214（4A）:97

Surviving L 17.5 cm W 3.0 cm

Stage 1 of Hemudu culture

Unearthed from the Hemudu site in 1977

Collected in Zhejiang Provincial Museum

鎌形器

T214（4A）:97

残長 17.5 cm 幅 3.0 cm

河姆渡文化 1 期

1977 年河姆渡遺跡出土

浙江省博物館蔵

23

哨

左：T3（下）:20
长 5.3、直径 0.9 厘米
中:T21（4）:26
长 6.8、直径 0.9 厘米
右：T31（4）:54
外残长 5.5、内残长 8.4 厘米
河姆渡文化一期
1973 年河姆渡遗址出土
浙江省博物馆藏

WHISTLES

Left：T3（Lower）:20
L 5.3 cm D 0.9 cm
Middle：T21（4）:26
L 6.8 cm D 0.9 cm
Right：T31（4）:54
Surviving L 5.5 cm（outer）
Surviving L 8.4 cm（inner）
Stage 1 of Hemudu culture
Unearthed from the Hemudu site in 1973
Collected in Zhejiang Provincial Museum

哨（楽器）

左：T3（下）:20
長 5.3 cm 直径 0.9 cm
中：T21（4）:26
長 6.8 cm 直径 0.9 cm
右：T31（4）:54
残長（外）5.5 cm （内）8.4 cm
河姆渡文化 1 期
1973 年河姆渡遺跡出土
浙江省博物館蔵

24

镞

左 1：T211（4A）:233

残长 5.6、直径 1.2 厘米

左 2：T232（4A）:77

长 7.7、宽 0.9 厘米

中：T243（4A）:219

长 8.0、宽 1.0 厘米

右 2：T234（4B）:233

残长 8.8、直径 0.9 厘米

右 1：T224（4A）:63

长 15.3、直径 1.0 厘米

河姆渡文化一期

1977 年河姆渡遗址出土

河姆渡遗址博物馆藏

ARROWHEADS

Left 1：T211（4A）:233

Surviving L 5.6 cm　D 1.2 cm

Left 2：T232（4A）:77

L 7.7 cm　W 0.9 cm

Middle：T243（4A）:219

L 8.0 cm　W 1.0 cm

Right 2：T234（4B）:233

Surviving L 8.8 cm　D 0.9 cm

Right 1：T224（4A）:63

L 15.3 cm　D 1.0 cm

Stage 1 of Hemudu culture

Unearthed from the Hemudu site in 1977

Collected in the Museum of the Hemudu Site

鏃

左 1：T211（4A）:233

殘長 5.6 cm　直徑 1.2 cm

左 2：T232（4A）:77

長 7.7 cm　幅 0.9 cm

中：T243（4A）:219

長 8.0 cm　幅 1.0 cm

右 2：T234（4B）:233

殘長 8.8 cm　直徑 0.9 cm

右 1：T224（4A）:63

長 15.3 cm　直徑 1.0 cm

河姆渡文化 1 期

1977 年河姆渡遺跡出土

河姆渡遺址博物館藏

25

鱼镖

T242（4）:305

长 8.6 厘米

河姆渡文化一期

1977 年河姆渡遗址出土

浙江省博物馆藏

AIR BLADDER

T242（4）:305

L 8.6 cm

Stage 1 of Hemudu culture

Unearthed from the Hemudu site in 1977

Collected in Zhejiang Provincial Museum

魚銛

T242（4）:305

長 8.6 cm

河姆渡文化 1 期

1977 年河姆渡遺跡出土

浙江省博物館蔵

26

凿

左：T244（4A）:171

长 5.8、宽 1.5、厚 0.7 厘米

右：T226（4A）:164

长 13.1、刃宽 0.7 厘米

河姆渡文化一期

1977 年河姆渡遗址出土

河姆渡遗址博物馆藏

CHISELS

Left：T244（4A）:171

L 5.8 cm　W 1.5 cm　T 0.7 cm

Right：T226（4A）:164

L 13.1 cm　W 0.7 cm（blade）

Stage 1 of Hemudu culture

Unearthed from the Hemudu site in 1977

Collected in the Museum of the Hemudu Site

鑿

左：T244（4A）:171

長 5.8 cm　幅 1.5 cm　厚さ0.7 cm

右：T226（4A）:164

長 13.1 cm　刃部幅 0.7 cm

河姆渡文化 1 期

1977 年河姆渡遺跡出土

河姆渡遺址博物館蔵

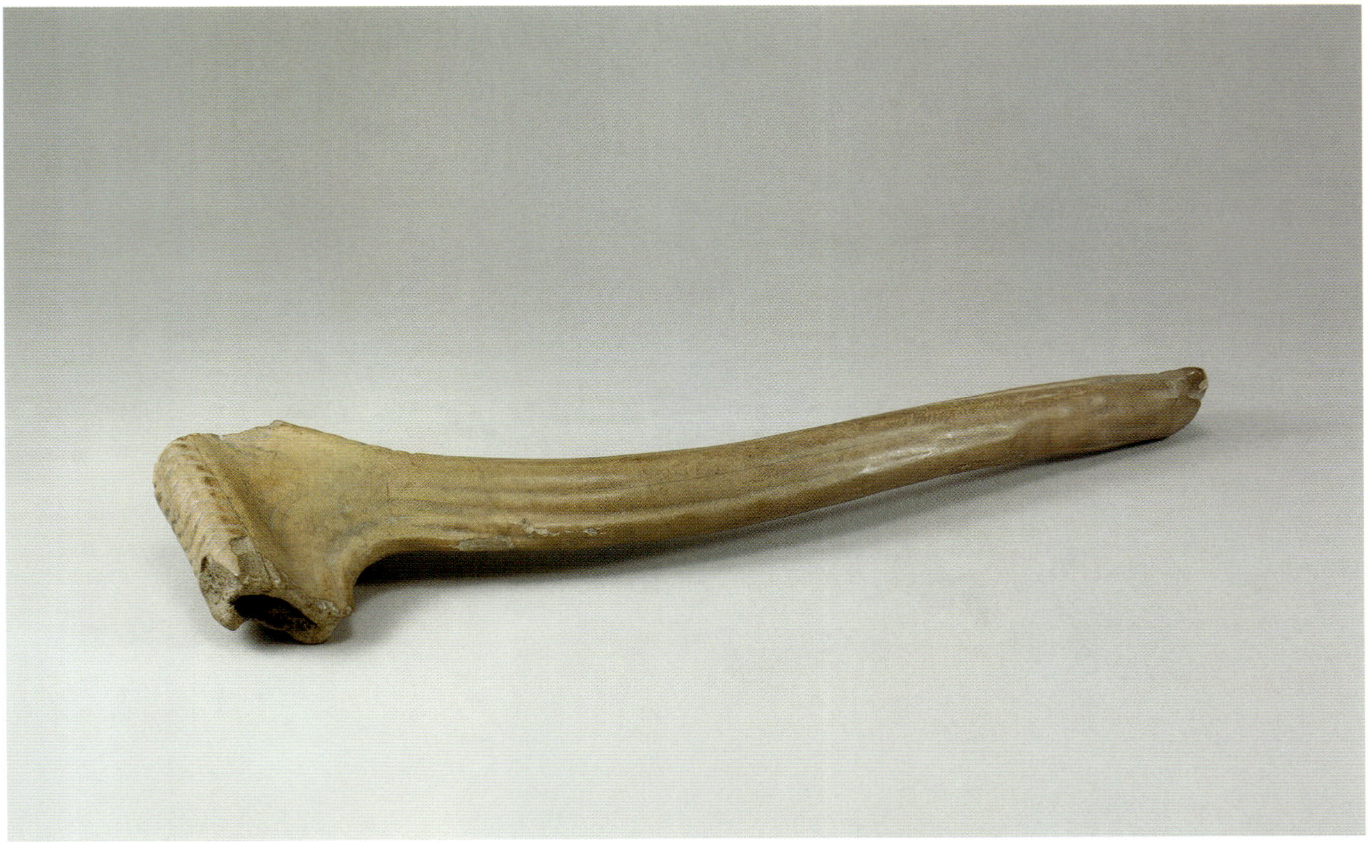

27

角斧柄
T212（4）:228
长叉长 40.5、
短叉残长 10.05 厘米
河姆渡文化一期
1977 年河姆渡遗址出土
浙江省博物馆藏

ANTLER SHAFT OF AXE
T212（4）:228
L 40.5 cm（longer fork）
Surviving L 10.05 cm（shorter fork）
Stage 1 of Hemudu culture
Unearthed from the Hemudu site in 1977
Collected in Zhejiang Provincial Museum

角製の斧の柄
T212（4）:228
柄部の長 40.5 cm
基部の残長 10.05 cm
河姆渡文化 1 期
1977 年河姆渡遺跡出土
浙江省博物館蔵

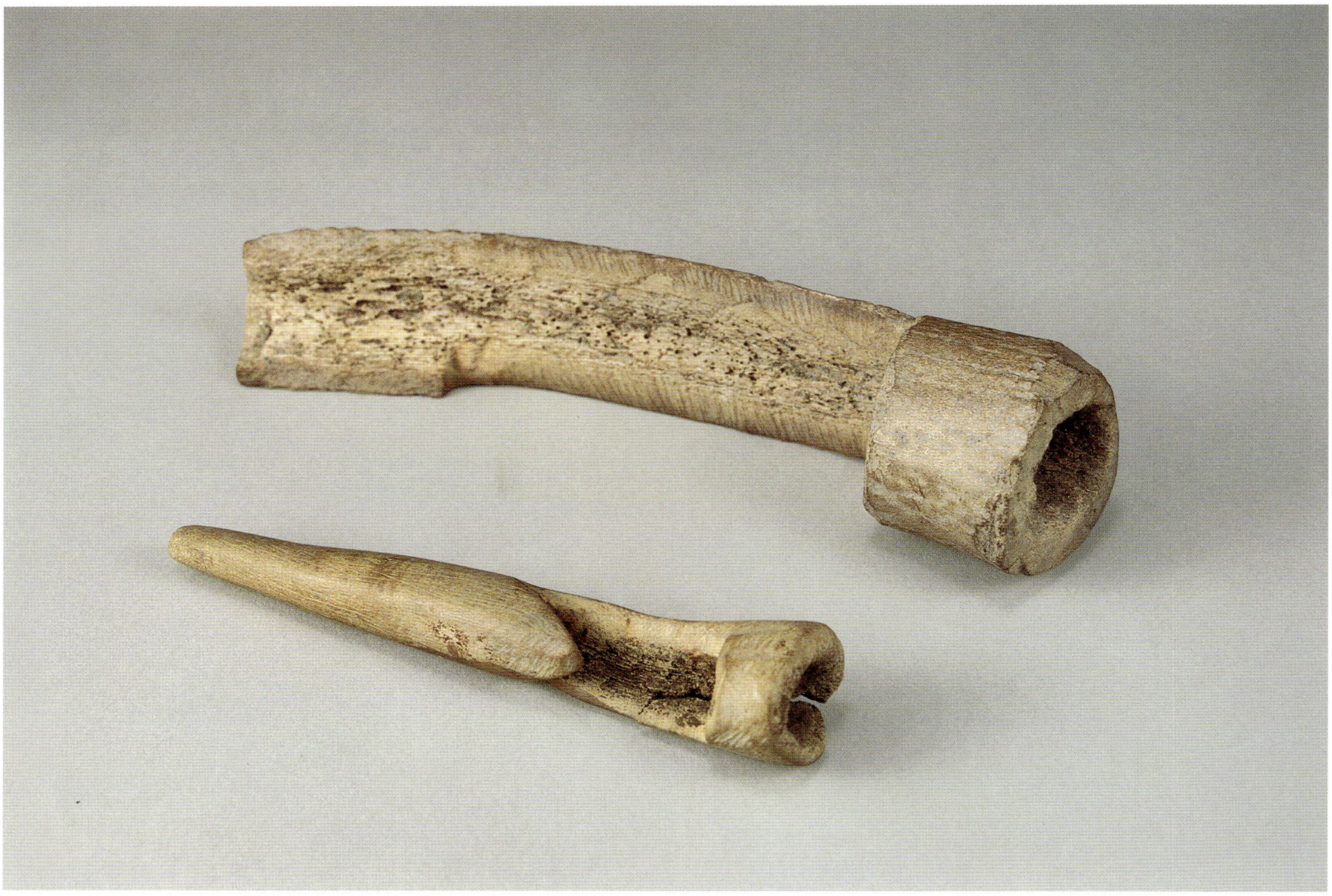

28

上：经轴

T234（4B）:266

长 13.3 厘米

下：梭形器

T211（4B）:404

长 9.7 厘米

河姆渡文化一期

1977 年河姆渡遗址出土

河姆渡遗址博物馆藏

UP：WARP ROLLER

T234（4B）:266

L 13.3 cm

LOW：SHUTTLE SHAPED TOOL

T211（4B）:404

L 9.7 cm

Stage 1 of Hemudu culture

Unearthed from the Hemudu site in 1977

Collected in the Museum of the Hemudu Site

上：経軸

T234（4B）:266

長 13.3 cm

下：梭形器

T211（4B）:404

長 9.7 cm

河姆渡文化 1 期

1977 年河姆渡遺跡出土

河姆渡遺址博物館藏

29

梭形器
T29（4）:56
长 23.5、直径 2.3 厘米
河姆渡文化一期
1973 年河姆渡遗址出土
浙江省博物馆藏

SHUTTLE SHAPED TOOL
T29（4）:56
L 23.5 cm　D 2.3 cm
Stage 1 of Hemudu culture
Unearthed from the Hemudu site in 1973
Collected in Zhejiang Provincial Museum

梭形器
T29（4）:56
長 23.5 cm　直徑 2.3 cm
河姆渡文化 1 期
1973 年河姆渡遺跡出土
浙江省博物館藏

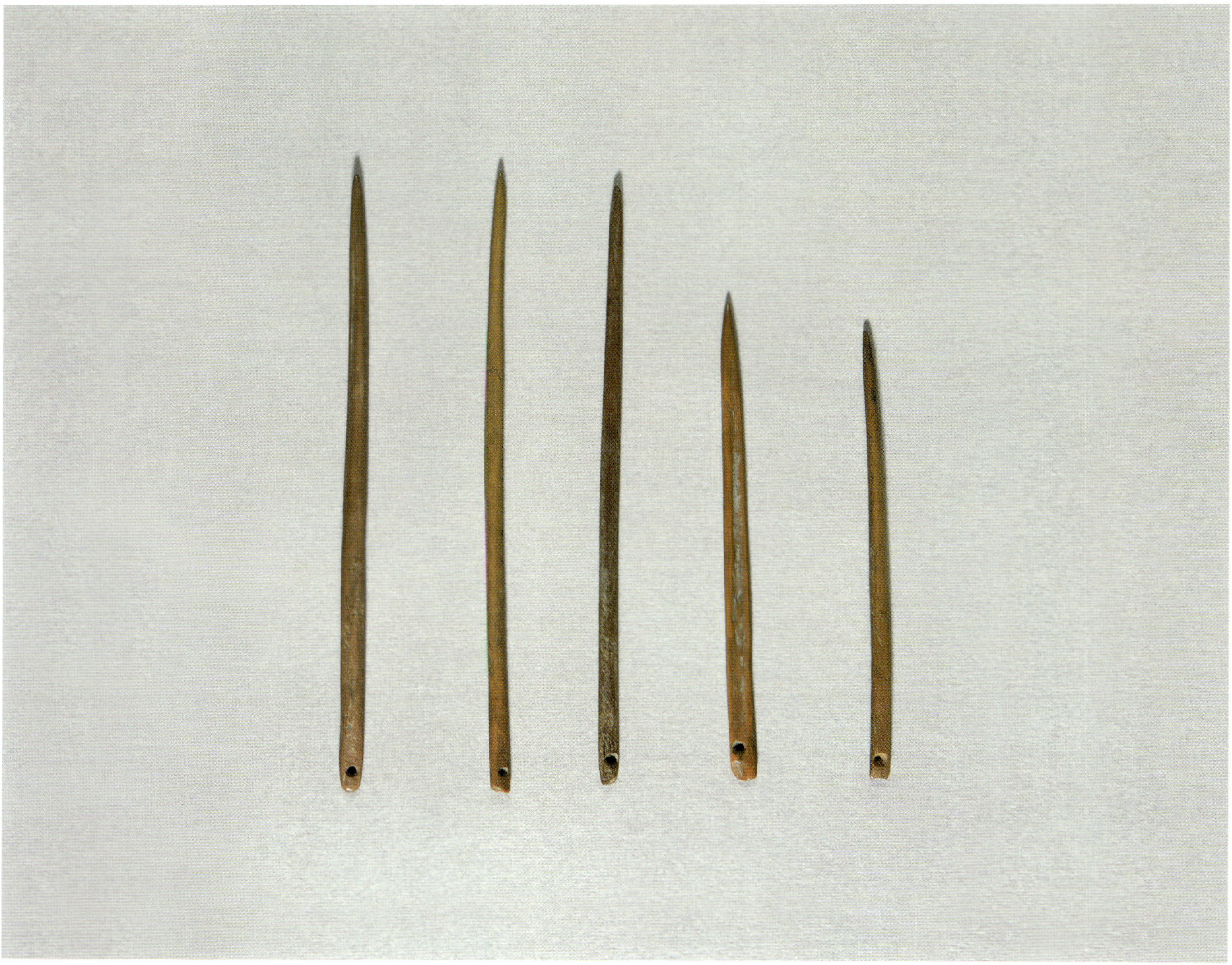

30

针

左 1：T211（3C）:104
长 9.1、直径 0.3 厘米
左 2：T242（4A）:215
长 9.0、直径 0.2 厘米
中： T242（4B）:353
长 8.7、直径 0.2 厘米
右 2：T211（4B）:304
长 6.9、直径 0.3 厘米
右 1：T221（4B）:379
长 6.5、直径 0.3 厘米
河姆渡文化一、二期
1977 年河姆渡遗址出土
河姆渡遗址博物馆藏

NEEDLES

Left 1：T211（3C）:104
L 9.1 cm D 0.3 cm
Left 2：T242（4A）:215
L 9.0 cm D 0.2 cm
Middle：T242（4B）:353
L 8.7 cm D 0.2 cm
Right 2：T211（4B）:304
L 6.9 cm D 0.3 cm
Right 1：T211（4B）:379
L 6.5 cm D 0.3 cm
Stages 1 and 2 of Hemudu culture
Unearthed from the Hemudu site in 1977
Collected in the Museum of the Hemudu Site

針

左 1：T211（3C）:104
長 9.1 cm 直徑 0.3 cm
左 2：T242（4A）:215
長 9.0 cm 直徑 0.2 cm
中：T242（4B）:353
長 8.7 cm 直徑 0.2 cm
右 2：T211（4B）:304
長 6.9 cm 直徑 0.3 cm
右 1：T221（4B）:379
長 6.5 cm 直徑 0.3 cm
河姆渡文化 1、2 期
1977 年河姆渡遺跡出土
河姆渡遺址博物館藏

31
管状针
左：T226（3B）:55
长 14.0、直径 0.5 厘米
右：T224（4A）:122
长 16.2、直径 0.6 厘米
河姆渡文化一、二期
1977 年河姆渡遗址出土
河姆渡遗址博物馆藏

TUBULAR NEEDLES
Left：T226（3B）:55
L 14.0 cm　D 0.5 cm
Right：T224（4A）:22
L 16.2 cm　D 0.6 cm
Stages 1 and 2 of Hemudu culture
Unearthed from the Hemudu site in 1977
Collected in the Museum of the Hemudu Site

管狀針
左：T226（3B）:55
長 14.0 cm　直徑 0.5 cm
右：T224（4A）:122
長 16.2 cm　直徑 0.6 cm
河姆渡文化 1、2 期
1977 年河姆渡遺跡出土
河姆渡遺址博物館藏

32

圆雕鸟形象牙匕
T244（4A）:124
长 15.8、宽 3.4、厚 0.8 厘米
河姆渡文化一期
1977 年河姆渡遗址出土
中国历史博物馆藏

IVORY DAGGER SCULPTED IN BIRD SHAPE
T244（4A）:124
L 15.8 cm W 3.4 cm T 0.8 cm
Stage 1 of Hemudu culture
Unearthed from the Hemudu site in 1977
Collected in National Museum of Chinese History

象牙鳥形匕（丸彫り）
T244（4A）:124
長 15.8 cm 幅 3.4 cm 厚さ0.8 cm
河姆渡文化 1 期
1977 年河姆渡遺跡出土
中国歴史博物館蔵

33

圆雕鸟形象牙匕

长 15.5、宽 2.6、厚 1.4 厘米

河姆渡文化一期

1977 年河姆渡遗址出土

河姆渡遗址博物馆藏

IVORY DAGGER SCULPTED IN BIRD SHAPE

L 15.5 cm　W 2.6 cm　T 1.4 cm

Stage 1 of Hemudu culture

Unearthed from the Hemudu site in 1977

Collected in the Museum of the Hemudu Site

象牙鳥形匕（丸彫り）

長 15.5 cm　幅 2.6 cm　厚さ1.4 cm

河姆渡文化 1 期

1977 年河姆渡遺跡出土

河姆渡遺址博物館蔵

34

圆雕鸟形象牙匕

T8（9）:30

长 13.6 厘米

河姆渡文化一期

1996 年鲻山遗址出土

浙江省文物考古研究所藏

IVORY DAGGER SCULPTED IN BIRD SHAPE

T8（9）:30

L 13.6 cm

Stage 1 of Hemudu culture

Unearthed from the Zishan site in 1996

Collected in Zhejiang Provincial Institute of Cultural Relics and Archaeology

象牙鳥形匕（丸彫り）

T8（9）:30

長 13.6 cm

河姆渡文化 1 期

1996 年鯔山遺跡出土

浙江省文物考古研究所藏

35

双鸟纹匕柄
T21（4）:18
长 14.5、宽 3.4 厘米
河姆渡文化一期
1973 年河姆渡遗址出土
浙江省博物馆藏

SHAFT OF DAGGER CARVED WITH DOUBLE BIRDS
T21（4）:18
L 14.5 cm　W 3.4 cm
Stage 1 of Hemudu culture
Unearthed from the Hemudu site in 1973
Collected in Zhejiang Provincial Museum

双鳥文匕柄
T21（4）:18
長 14.5 cm　幅 3.4 cm
河姆渡文化 1 期
1973 年河姆渡遺跡出土
浙江省博物館蔵

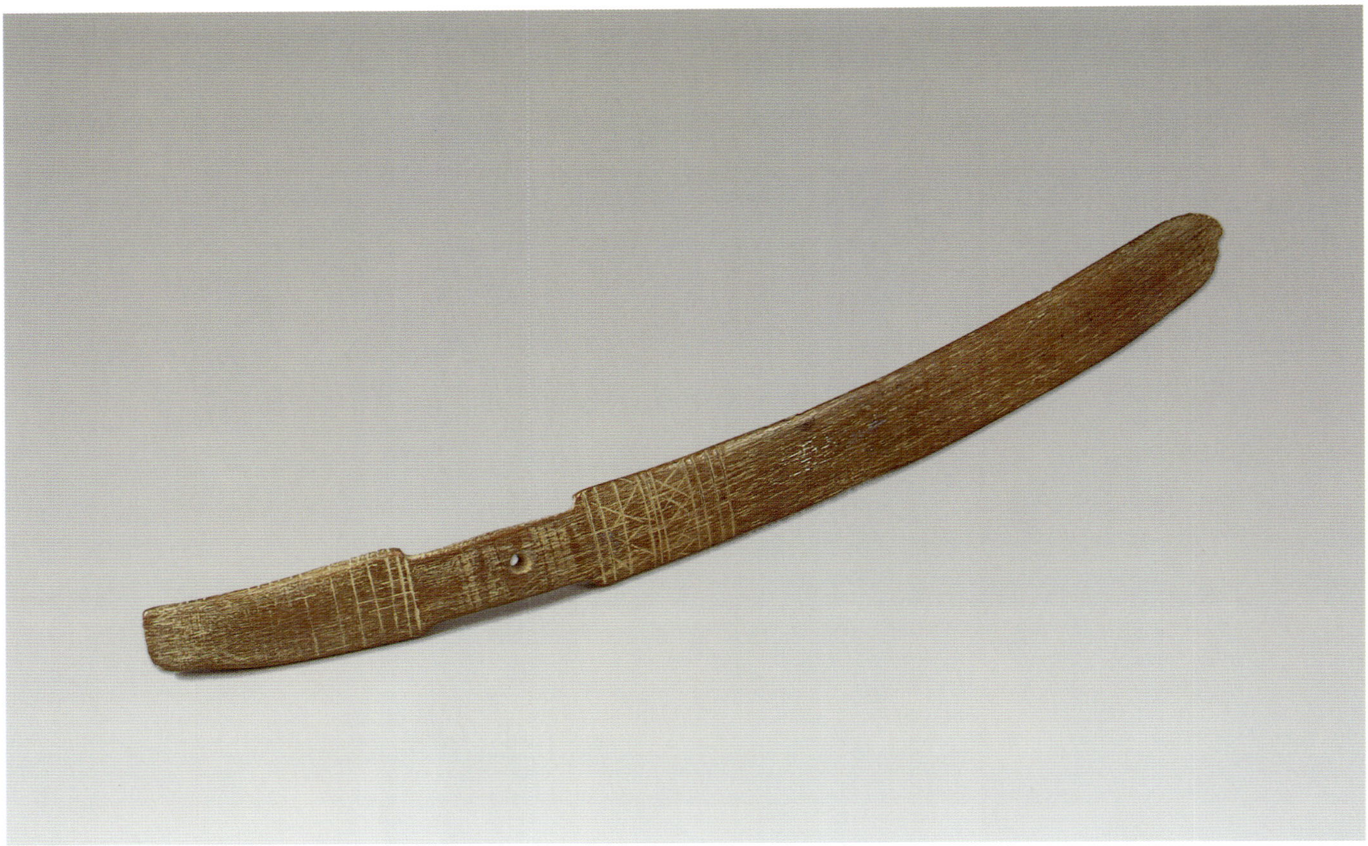

36

刻花匕
T213（4B）:116
长 26.4、宽 2.0、厚 0.4 厘米
河姆渡文化一期
1977 年河姆渡遗址出土
河姆渡遗址博物馆藏

CARVED DAGGER
T213（4B）:116
L 26.4 cm　W 2.0 cm　T 0.4 cm
Stage 1 of Hemudu culture
Unearthed from the Hemudu site in 1977
Collected in the Museum of the Hemudu Site

線刻のあるヒ
T213（4B）:116
長 26.4 cm　幅 2.0 cm　厚さ0.4 cm
河姆渡文化 1 期
1977 年河姆渡遺跡出土
河姆渡遺址博物館蔵

37

匙

T231（3）:25

长 13、匙身宽 3.5、

柄宽 1、厚 0.2 厘米

河姆渡文化二期

1977 年河姆渡遗址出土

浙江省博物馆藏

DAGGER

T231（3）:25

L 13 cm　W 3.5 cm（dagger）

W 1 cm（shaft）　T 0.2 cm

Stage 2 of Hemudu culture

Unearthed from the Hemudu site in 1977

Collected in Zhejiang Provincial Museum

匙

T231（3）:25

長 13 cm　幅 3.5 cm

柄の幅 1 cm　厚さ0.2 cm

河姆渡文化 2 期

1977 年河姆渡遺跡出土

浙江省博物館藏

38

太阳纹象牙蝶形器

T224（3B）:82

残长 8.3、残宽 5.4、厚 0.9 厘米

河姆渡文化二期

1977 年河姆渡遗址出土

河姆渡遗址博物馆藏

IVORY BUTTERFLY-SHAPED ORNAMENT WITH THE SUN DESIGN

T224（3B）:82

Surviving L 8.3 cm, surviving W 5.4 cm, T 1.2 cm

Stage 2 of Hemudu culture

Unearthed from the Hemudu site in 1977

Collected in the Museum of the Hemudu Site

太陽文象牙蝶形器

T224（3B）:82

残長 8.3 cm　残幅 5.4 cm　厚さ0.9 cm

河姆渡文化 2 期

1977 年河姆渡遺跡出土

河姆渡遺址博物館蔵

39

双鸟朝阳纹象牙蝶形器
T226（3B）:79
长 16.6、残宽 5.9、厚 1.2 厘米
河姆渡文化二期
1977 年河姆渡遗址出土
浙江省博物馆藏

IVORY BUTTERFLY-SHAPED ORNAMENT WITH DOUBLE BIRDS FACED THE SUN
T226（3B）:79
L 16.6 cm　surviving W 5.9 cm　T 1.2 cm
Stage 2 of Hemudu culture
Unearthed from the Hemudu site in 1977
Collected in Zhejiang Provincial Museum

双鳥朝陽文象牙蝶形器
T226（3B）:79
長 16.6 cm　残幅 5.9 cm　厚さ1.2 cm
河姆渡文化 2 期
1977 年河姆渡遺跡出土
浙江省博物館蔵

40

象牙盖帽形器
T244（3）:71
口径 4.8、高 3.5 厘米
河姆渡文化二期
1977 年河姆渡遗址出土
浙江省博物馆藏

IVORY LID-SHAPED ARTIFACT
T244（3）:71
D 4.8 cm（m） H 3.5 cm
Stage 2 of Hemudu culture
Unearthed from the Hemudu site in 1977
Collected in Zhejiang Provincial Museum

象牙蓋形器
T244（3）:71
口徑 4.8 cm　高 3.5 cm
河姆渡文化 2 期
1977 年河姆渡遺跡出土
浙江省博物館藏

41

笄
T213（3B）:53
长 11.4 厘米
河姆渡文化二期
1977 年河姆渡遗址出土
河姆渡遗址博物馆藏

HAIRPIN
T213（3B）:53
L 11.4 cm
Stage 2 of Hemudu culture
Unearthed from the Hemudu site in 1977
Collected in the Museum of the Hemudu Site

笄
T213（3B）:53
長 11.4 cm
河姆渡文化 2 期
1977 年河姆渡遺跡出土
河姆渡遺址博物館蔵

42

珠

左：T233（4B）:195

直径 2.6 厘米

右：T242（4A）:255

直径 3.7 厘米

河姆渡文化一期

1977 年河姆渡遗址出土

河姆渡遗址博物馆藏

BEADS

Left：T233（4B）:195

D 2.6 cm

Right：T242（4A）:225

D 3.7 cm

Stage 1 of Hemudu culture

Unearthed from the Hemudu site in 1977

Collected in the Museum of the Hemudu Site

珠

左：T233（4B）:195

直径 2.6 cm

右：T242（4A）:255

直径 3.7 cm

河姆渡文化 1 期

1977 年河姆渡遺跡出土

河姆渡遺址博物館蔵

43

左：牙坠饰

T235（3A）:40

长 6.3、厚 0.5 厘米

右：坠饰

T223（4A）:99

长 2.9、厚 0.5 厘米

河姆渡文化一、二期

1977 年河姆渡遗址出土

河姆渡遗址博物馆藏

Left：**TOOTH PENDANT**

T235（3A）:40

L 6.3 cm　T 0.5 cm

Left：**PENDANT**

T223（4A）:99

L 2.9 cm　T 0.5 cm

Stages 1 and 2 of Hemudu culture

Unearthed from the Hemudu site in 1977

Collected in the Museum of the Hemudu Site

左：牙製飾り

T235（3A）:40

長 6.3 cm　厚さ0.5 cm

右：飾り

T223（4A）:99

長 2.9 cm　厚さ0.5 cm

河姆渡文化 1、2 期

1977 年河姆渡遺跡出土

河姆渡遺址博物館蔵

44

角坠饰
T233（4B）:194
长 8.8 厘米
河姆渡文化一期
1977 年河姆渡遗址出土
河姆渡遗址博物馆藏

ANTLER ORNAMENT
T233（4B）:194
L 8.8 cm
Stage 1 of Hemudu culture
Unearthed from the Hemudu site in 1977
Collected in the Museum of the Hemudu Site

角製飾り
T233（4B）:194
長 8.8 cm
河姆渡文化 1 期
1977 年河姆渡遺跡出土
河姆渡遺址博物館蔵

木　器

Wooden Implements

木　器

广泛使用木器又是河姆渡文化的一大特点。在河姆渡遗址中木器出土数量众多，器形丰富，且制作技术已达到相当高的水平。以用途可分为生产工具、生活用具、装饰物件，大多发现于河姆渡遗址第一、二期文化，尤以距地下三四米深的第一期文化为最多。器形有耜、铲、桨、矛（镞）、杋刀、卷布棍、匕、经轴、锯形器、纺轮、筒、杵、碗、陀螺、盘、槌、斧（锛）柄、蝶形器等等。其中的碗、筒等已运用了髹漆工艺。

The great wealth of wood implements is another feature of the Hemudu culture. A large number of wood implements is recovered from the Hemudu site in many shapes and the handcraft has reached advanced level. According to their function, they can be categorized into productive tools, daily utensils, and ornaments. Most of them were found in stages 1 and 2 of the Hemudu culture, especially rich in stage 1 which deposited 3-4 meters deep beneath the surface ground. The types include hoe blades, spatulas, oars, spears (arrowheads), knives, small sticks, warp pegs, saw-shaped tool, spindle whorls, tubes, pestles, bowls, tops, plates, mallets, shafts of axes (adzes) and butterfly-shaped ware. The above mentioned bowls and tubes are painted.

広範な木器の使用は河姆渡文化の特徴の一つである。河姆渡遺跡では木器の出土量が比較的多く器種も豊富で、なおかつ製作技術は相当高いレベルにあった。用途によって生産工具、生活用具、装飾品に分けられ、ほとんどが河姆渡遺跡第1期、2期文化に見られる。中でも地下3～4mの第1期文化に最も多い。器種は耜、鏟、櫂、矛（鏃）、緯打具、布巻き具、匕、経軸、鋸形器、紡錘車、筒、杵、碗、コマ、盤、槌、斧（手斧）、柄、蝶形器などである。その中で碗、筒などには漆が使われた。

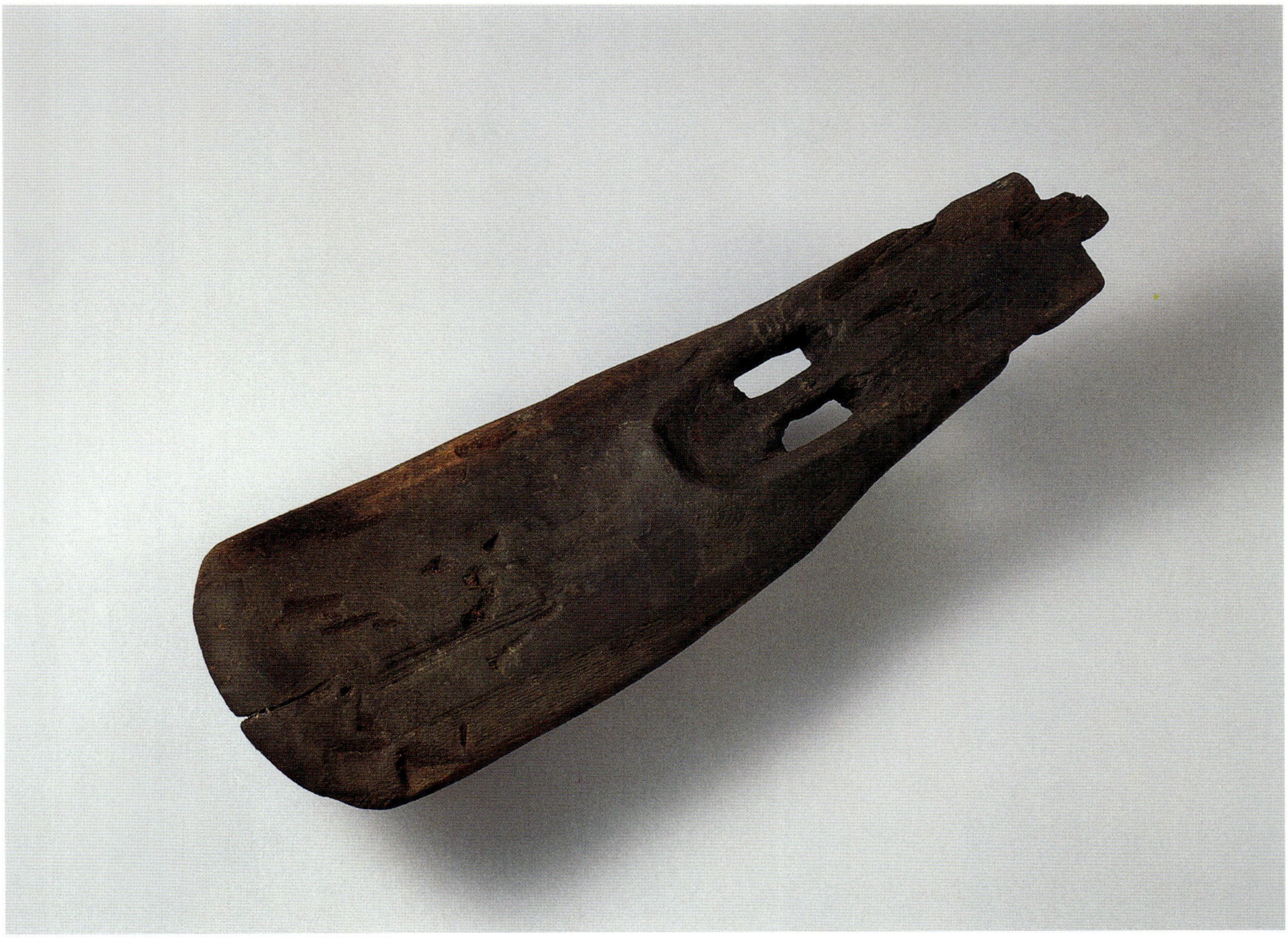

45

耜

T10（9）:8

长 36.7 厘米

河姆渡文化一期

1996 年鲻山遗址出土

浙江省文物考古研究所藏

SI **- SPADE**

T10（9）:8

L 36.7 cm

Stage 1 of Hemudu culture

Unearthed from the Zishan site in 1996

Collected in Zhejiang Provincial Institute of Cultural Relics and Archaeology

耜

T10（9）:8

長 36.7 cm

河姆渡文化 1 期

1996 年鯔山遺跡出土

浙江省文物考古研究所蔵

46

耜

J1:7

长 36.0、刃宽 16.5、厚 1.5 厘米

河姆渡文化三期

1973 年河姆渡遗址出土

***SI* – SPADE**

J1:7

L 36.0 cm　W 15.5 cm (blade)　T 1.5 cm

Stage 3 of Hemudu culture

Unearthed from the Hemudu site in 1973

耜

J1:7

長 36.0 cm　刃部幅 16.5 cm　厚 1.5 cm

河姆渡文化 3 期

1973 年河姆渡遺跡出土

47

耜

T202（下）:11

长 31.0、刃宽 16.5 厘米

河姆渡文化四期

1988 年慈湖遗址出土

浙江省文物考古研究所藏

SI **– SPADE**

T202（Lower）:11

L 31.0 cm　W 16.5 cm（blade）

Stage 4 of Hemudu culture

Unearthed from the Cihu site in 1988

Collected in Zhejiang Provincial Institute of Cultural Relics and Archaeology

耜

T202（下）:11

長 31.0 cm　刃部幅 16.5 cm

河姆渡文化 4 期

1988 年慈湖遺跡出土

浙江省文物考古研究所蔵

48

镞
T502（下）:1
残长 10.7 厘米
河姆渡文化四期
1988 年慈湖遗址出土
浙江省文物考古研究所藏

ARROWHEAD
T502 (Lower):1
Surviving L 10.7 cm
Stage 4 of Hemudu culture
Unearthed from the Cihu site in 1988
Collected in Zhejiang Provincial Institute of Cultural Relics and Archaeology

鏃
T502（下）:1
殘長 10.7 cm
河姆渡文化 4 期
1988 年河慈湖遺跡出土
浙江省文物考古研究所藏

49

斧柄	SHAFT OF AXE	斧の柄
T212（4B）:243	T212（4B）:243	T212（4B）:243
通长 28.0、头宽 14.0 厘米	L 28.0 cm　W 14.0 cm（top）	長 28.0 cm　（基部）幅 14.0 cm
河姆渡文化一期	Stage 1 of Hemudu culture	河姆渡文化 1 期
1977 年河姆渡遗址出土	Unearthed from the Hemudu site in 1977	1977 年河姆渡遺跡出土

50

刻花器柄
T2（9）:13
残长 51.0、宽 3.4、厚 1.9 厘米
河姆渡文化一期
1996 年鲻山遗址出土
河姆渡遗址博物馆藏

SHAFT WITH CARVED DESIGN
T2（9）:13
Surviving L 51.0 cm　W 3.4 cm　T 1.9 cm
Stage 1 of Hemudu culture
Unearthed from the Zishan site in 1996
Collected in the Museum of the Hemudu Site

線刻のある柄
T2（9）:13
残長 51.0 cm　幅 3.4 cm　厚さ 1.9 cm
河姆渡文化 1 期
1996 年鯔山遺跡出土
河姆渡遺址博物館蔵

51

鱼形器柄

T231（4）:303

残长 17.7、宽 5.5、厚 0.3 厘米

河姆渡文化一期

1977 年河姆渡遗址出土

浙江省博物馆藏

FISH-SHAPED HANDLE

T231（4）:303

Surviving L 17.7 cm　W 5.5 cm　T 0.3 cm

Stage 1 of Hemudu culture

Unearthed from the Hemudu site in 1977

Collected in Zhejiang Provincial Museum

魚形柄

T231（4）:303

残長 17.7 cm　幅 5.5 cm　厚さ0.3 cm

河姆渡文化 1 期

1977 年河姆渡遺跡出土

浙江省博物館蔵

52
T字形器柄
残长 20.3、柄端宽 8.3 厘米
河姆渡文化一期
1996 年鲻山遗址出土
河姆渡遗址博物馆藏

T-SHAPED HANDLE
Surviving L 20.3 cm　W 8.3 cm（shaft）
Stage 1 of Hemudu culture
Unearthed from the Zishan site in 1996
Collected in the Museum of the Hemudu Site

T 字形柄
残長 20.3 cm　柄端部の幅 8.3 cm
河姆渡文化 1 期
1996 年鲻山遺跡出土
河姆渡遺址博物館蔵

53

杵

T233（4A）:115

长 92.0、杵头径 8.3、柄径 5.0 厘米

河姆渡文化一期

1977 年河姆渡遗址出土

浙江省博物馆藏

PESTLE

T233（4A）:115

L 92.0 cm　D 8.3 cm（top）　D 5.0 cm（shaft）

Stage 1 of Hemudu culture

Unearthed from the Hemudu site in 1977

Collected in Zhejiang Provincial Museum

杵

T233（4A）:115

長 92.0 cm　頂部の径 8.3 cm　柄の径 5.0 cm

河姆渡文化 1 期

1977 年河姆渡遺跡出土

浙江省博物館蔵

54
槌
T231（3B）:23
长 28.5、槌头高 6、槌面宽 8.4 厘米
河姆渡文化二期
1977 年河姆渡遗址出土

MALLET
T231（3B）:23
L 28.5 cm　H 6 cm（top）　W 8.4 cm
Stage 2 of Hemudu culture
Unearthed from the Hemudu site in 1977

槌
T231（3B）:23
長 28.5 cm　槌の高 6 cm　槌面の幅 8.4 cm
河姆渡文化 2 期
1977 年河姆渡遺跡出土

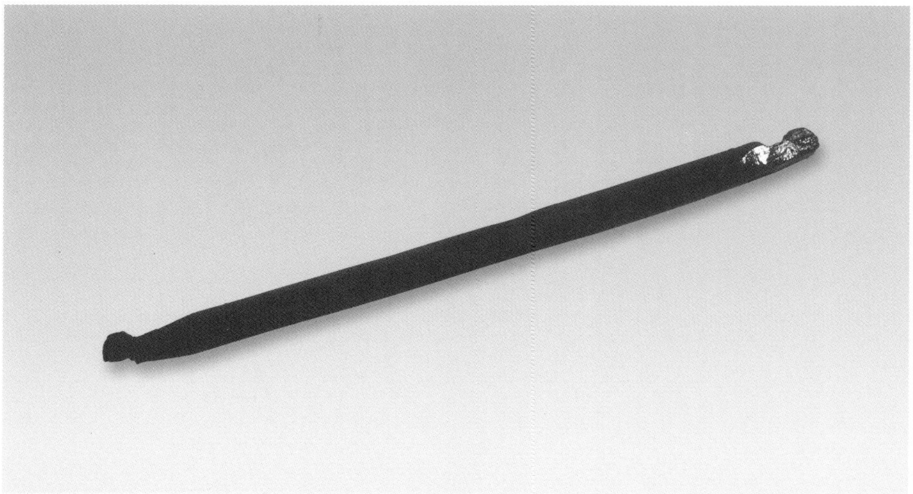

55
卷布棍
T18（4）:47
残长 17 厘米
河姆渡文化一期
1973 年河姆渡遗址出土

STICK FOR ROLLING CLOTH
T18（4）:47
Surviving L 17 cm
Stage 1 of Hemudu culture
Unearthed from the Hemudu site in 1973

布巻き具
T18（4）:47
残長 17 cm
河姆渡文化 1 期
1973 年河姆渡遺跡出土

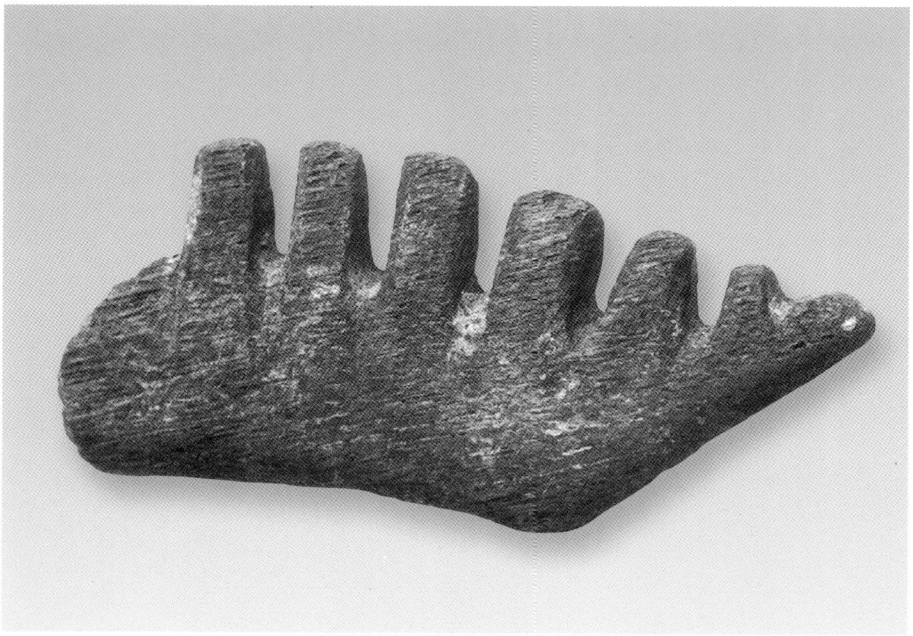

56
锯形器
T222（4A）:153
残长 7.6、宽 2.6、厚 0.7 厘米
河姆渡文化一期
1977 年河姆渡遗址出土

TOOTH-SHAPED ARTIFACT
T222（4A）:153
Surviving L 7.6 cm　W 2.6 cm　T 0.7 cm
Stage 1 of Hemudu culture
Unearthed from the Hemudu site in 1973

鋸形器
T222（4A）:153
残高 7.6 cm　幅 2.6 cm　厚さ 0.7 cm
河姆渡文化 1 期
1977 年河姆渡遺跡出土

57

刀

T231（4A）:174

通长 23.6、柄长 17.7、刀宽 3.7 厘米

河姆渡文化一期

1977 年河姆渡遗址出土

浙江省博物馆藏

KNIFE

T231（4A）:174

L 23.6 cm　L 17.7 cm（shaft）　W 3.7 cm（blade）

Stage 1 of Hemudu culture

Unearthed from the Hemudu site in 1977

Collected in Zhejiang Provincial Museum

刀

T231（4A）:174

長 23.6 cm　柄部長 17.7 cm　刀部幅 3.7 cm

河姆渡文化 1 期

1977 年河姆渡遺跡出土

浙江省博物館蔵

58

桨

T221（4A）:181

残长 62.0、柄宽 3.5、

桨叶长 27.8、厚 2.0 厘米

河姆渡文化一期

1977 年河姆渡遗址出土

OAR

T221（4A）:181

Surviving L 62.0 cm W 3.5 cm（shaft），

L 27.8 cm（oar body） T 2.0 cm（oar）

Stage 1 of Hemudu culture

Unearthed from the Hemudu site in 1977

櫂

T221（4A）:181

残長 62.0 cm 柄の幅 3.5 cm

葉形部の長 27.8 cm 葉形部の厚さ2.0 cm

河姆渡文化 1 期

1977 年河姆渡遺跡出土

59

漆碗
T231（3B）:30
高 5.7、口径 10.6～9.2、
底径 7.6～7.2 厘米
河姆渡文化二期
1977 年河姆渡遺址出土
浙江省博物馆藏

LACQUER BOWL
T231（3B）:30
H 5.7 cm　D 10.6－9.2 cm（m）
D 6－7.2 cm（b）
Stage 2 of Hemudu culture
Unearthed from the Hemudu site in 1977
Collected in Zhejiang Provincial Museum

漆碗
T231（3B）:30
高 5.7 cm　口径 10.6～9.2 cm
底径 7.6～7.2 cm
河姆渡文化 2 期
1977 年河姆渡遺跡出土
浙江省博物館藏

60

圆雕鱼
T231（4B）:309
长 10.2、宽 3.5、厚 2.7 厘米
河姆渡文化一期
1977 年河姆渡遗址出土
浙江省博物馆藏

FISH
T231（4B）:309
L 10.2 cm　W 3.5 cm　T 2.7 cm
Stage 1 of Hemudu culture
Unearthed from the Hemudu site in 1977
Collected in Zhejiang Provincial Museum

魚（丸彫り）
T231（4B）:309
長 10.2 cm　幅 3.5 cm　厚さ2.7 cm
河姆渡文化 1 期
1977 年河姆渡遺跡出土
浙江省博物館蔵

61

蝶形器

T17（4）:37

长 23.0、宽 13.5 厘米

河姆渡文化一期

1973 年河姆渡遗址出土

浙江省博物馆藏

BUTTERFLY-SHAPED ORNAMENT

T17（4）:37

L 23.0 cm　W 13.5 cm

Stage 1 of Hemudu culture

Unearthed from the Hemudu site in 1973

Collected in Zhejiang Provincial Museum

蝶形器

T17（4）:37

長 23.0 cm　幅 13.5 cm

河姆渡文化 1 期

1973 年河姆渡遺跡出土

浙江省博物館藏

62

筒

T3（9）:6

长 32、大端直径 12、小端直径 10.4 厘米

河姆渡文化一期

1996 年鲻山遗址出土

河姆渡遗址博物馆藏

BUCKET

T3（9）:6

L 32 cm　D 12 cm（major）　D 10.4 cm（minor）

Stage 1 of Hemudu culture

Unearthed from the Zishan site in 1996

Collected in the Museum of the Hemudu Site

筒

T3（9）:6

長 32 cm　端部直径（広）12 cm　（狭）10.4 cm

河姆渡文化 1 期

1996 年鯔山遺跡出土

河姆渡遺址博物館蔵

63
髹漆筒
T17（4）:23
长 32.6、外径 9.4、壁厚 0.7 厘米
河姆渡文化一期
1973 年河姆渡遗址出土
浙江省博物馆藏

PAINTED BUCKET
T17（4）:23
L 32.6 cm　D 9.4 cm（outer）　T 0.7 cm
Stage 1 of Hemudu culture
Unearthed from the Hemudu site in 1973
Collected in Zhejiang Provincial Museum

漆塗りの筒
T17（4）:23
長 32.6 cm　径 9.4 cm　器壁の厚さ0.7 cm
河姆渡文化 1 期
1973 年河姆渡遺跡出土
浙江省博物館蔵

陶　器

Pottery Wares

土　器

河姆渡文化陶器主要是生活用具。第一期陶器分夹炭黑陶、夹砂黑陶和彩陶三种陶系，器形有釜、罐、盆、盘、钵、豆、盂等。第二期仍以夹炭陶、夹砂陶为主，主要器形仍沿袭前期，新出现了灶和甑。第三期以夹砂灰陶为主，其次是夹砂红陶和泥质红陶，还有一定数量的夹炭红衣和夹炭灰衣陶，并有极少量的泥质黑陶。主要器类变化不大，增加了三足器。第四期陶系以夹砂红陶为主，器类与第三期同。

河姆渡文化第一、二期陶器多采用泥条盘筑分段拼接的制作方法，第三期以后出现慢轮修整技术。绳纹始终是河姆渡文化炊器上的最主要的装饰花纹。刻划纹主要是动物纹、植物纹以及由动植物演变而来的圈点和线条组成的各式图案花纹，变化复杂，以第一期最为明显。以后花纹装饰由繁到简，渐趋衰落，直至以素面为主。

河姆渡文化陶器除上述生活用具外，还有纺轮、陶塑动物形象、刻纹陶块、支架、陀螺、环、珠、丸及模拟实用生活器皿的小陶玩等。

The pottery of the Hemudu culture is mainly of daily utensils. The paste of stage 1 consists of carbon tempered and sandy black pottery and painted pottery, which include *fu*-cauldrons, *guan*-jars, *pen*-basins, *pan*-plates, *bo*-bowls, *dou*-stemmed bowls, and *yu*-vessels. In stage 2, the paste tempered with carbon and sand was dominant, stoves and *zeng*-steamers were added to the assemblage. In stage 3, sandy gray pottery is popular, sandy red wares and clay paste wares come the second. A number of carbon tempered wares coated with a layer of red and gray clay wash occurred. The clay paste black pottery is rare. The assemblage changed slightly, three-footed wares appeared. In stage 4, sandy red pottery is predominant, the assemblage is the same as that of stage 3.

In stages 1 and 2, pottery is handmade by spirally connecting clay slips together, and then trimmed by slow wheel in stage 3. Cord mark is the most popular design impressed on the cooking pots of the Hemudu culture. Decoration on pottery vessels is various and complicated with most of them as the incised design. Animals, plants and various patterns of animals and plants formed by dots and lines are the subject for decoration, particularly in stage 1. The trend of decoration is from complicated to simple, and finally become plain on the surface.

Besides the above mentioned daily pottery, we also found spindle whorls, clay animal sculptures, incised pottery shards, pot supports, tops, rings, beads, pills and small toys imitated from the daily wares.

河姆渡文化の土器は、主に生活用器である。第１期の土器は夾炭黒陶、夾砂黒陶と彩文土器の3種類に分けられる。器種は釜、罐、盆、鉢、豆、盂などである。第２期は依然として夾炭陶、夾砂陶が主であり、主要な器種は前期を踏襲しており、灶と甑が新しく出現する。第３期も夾砂陶が主で、その次に夾砂紅陶と泥質紅陶、そして一定量の夾炭紅衣陶と夾炭灰衣陶がある。さらにごく少量の泥質黒陶がある。主要な器種に大きな変化はなく、三足器が増加する。第 4 期は夾砂紅陶が主で、器種は第 3 期と同様である。

河姆渡文化第 1 期、2 期の土器は多くが粘土紐積み上げによって製作されている。第 3 期以降は回転台による調整技法が出現している。縄蓆文は終始河姆渡文化の煮沸容器の最も主要な装飾文様である。刻線文は主に動物文、植物文と、動植物が変化し円と線が組み合った各図案文様であり、変化が複雑で、第 1 期にもっとも顕著である。以後文様は簡素化し、次第に衰退して最後には無文が主となる。

河姆渡文化の土器は上述の生活用具以外に、紡錘車、動物をかたどった像、刻文陶塊、支脚、コマ、環、珠、球および生活用具を模倣した玩具などがある。

64

纺轮

左：T226（4A）:101（凸字形）

厚 3.0、面径 3.0、底径 4.4 厘米

右：T235（4A）:102（扁圆形）

直径 6.4、厚 1.0 厘米

河姆渡文化一期

1977 年河姆渡遗址出土

浙江省博物馆藏

SPINDLE WHORL

Left: T226 (4A):101

T 3.0 cm D 3.0 cm (top) D 4.4 cm (bottom)

Right: T235 (4A):102

D 6.4 cm T 1.0 cm

Stage 1 of Hemudu culture

Unearthed from the Hemudu site in 1977

Collected in Zhejiang Provincial Museum

紡錘車

左：T226（4A）:101（凸字形）

厚 3.0 cm 面径 3.0 cm 底径 4.4 cm

右：T235（4A）:102（楕円形）

直径 6.4 cm 厚さ1.0 cm

河姆渡文化 1 期

1977 年河姆渡遺跡出土

浙江省博物館蔵

65

拍

T243（2）:2

长 7.7、拍头径 6.2、柄径 4.2 厘米

河姆渡文化三期

1977 年河姆渡遗址出土

河姆渡遗址博物馆藏

PAT

T243（2）:2

L 7.7 cm　D 6.2 cm（top）　D 4.2 cm（shaft）

Stage 3 of Hemudu culture

Unearthed from the Hemudu site in 1977

Collected in the Museum of the Hemudu Site

拍（製作用の工具）

T243（2）:2

長 7.7 cm　頂径 6.2 cm　柄径 4.2 cm

河姆渡文化 3 期

1977 年河姆渡遺跡出土

河姆渡遺址博物館蔵

66

折敛口釜
T211（4A）:158
高 15.5、口径 16.7 厘米
河姆渡文化一期
1977 年河姆渡遗址出土
河姆渡遗址博物馆藏

***FU*－CAULDRON**
T211（4A）:158
H 15.5 cm　D 16.7 cm（m）
Stage 1 of Hemudu culture
Unearthed from the Hemudu site in 1977
Collected in the Museum of the Hemudu Site

折斂口釜
T211（4A）:158
高さ15.5 cm　口径 16.7 cm
河姆渡文化 1 期
1977 年河姆渡遺跡出土
河姆渡遺址博物館蔵

67

弧敛口筒腹釜

T11 (9):11

高 29.6、口径 20 厘米

河姆渡文化一期

1996 年鲻山遗址出土

河姆渡遗址博物馆藏

FU **- CAULDRON WITH BUCKET BODY**

T11 (9):11

H 29.6 cm D 20 cm (m)

Stage 1 of Hemudu culture

Unearthed from the Zishan site in 1996

Collected in the Museum of the Hemudu Site

弧斂口筒腹釜

T11 (9):11

高 29.6 cm 口徑 20 cm

河姆渡文化 1 期

1996 年鯔山遺跡出土

河姆渡遺址博物館藏

68

多角沿敛口釜
T26（4）:34
高 22.0、口径 22.4 厘米
河姆渡文化一期
1973 年河姆渡遗址出土
浙江省博物馆藏

***FU* - CAULDRON**
T26（4）:34
H 22.0 cm　D 22.4 cm（m）
Stage 1 of Hemudu culture
Unearthed from the Hemudu site in 1973
Collected in Zhejiang Provincial Museum

多角沿斂口釜
T26（4）:34
高 22.0 cm　口徑 22.4 cm
河姆渡文化 1 期
1973 年河姆渡遺跡出土
浙江省博物館蔵

69

敞口腰沿釜

T30（4）:75

残高 15.0、口径 17.1 厘米

河姆渡文化一期

1977 年河姆渡遗址出土

浙江省博物馆藏

***FU* - CAULDRON**

T30（4）:75

Surviving H 15.0 cm　D 17.1 cm（m）

Stage 1 of Hemudu culture

Unearthed from the Hemudu site in 1977

Collected in Zhejiang Provincial Museum

敞口腰沿釜

T30（4）:75

殘高 15.0 cm　口徑 17.1 cm

河姆渡文化 1 期

1977 年河姆渡遺跡出土

浙江省博物館藏

70

敞口釜

T9（9）:25

高 20.0、口径 21.6 厘米

河姆渡文化一期

1996 年鲻山遗址出土

河姆渡遗址博物馆藏

***FU* – CAULDRON**

T9（9）:25

H 20.0 cm　D 21.6 cm（m）

Stage 1 of Hemudu culture

Unearthed from the Zishan site in 1996

Collected in the Museum of the Hemudu Site

敞口釜

T9（9）:25

高 20.0 cm　口徑 21.6 cm

河姆渡文化 1 期

1996 年鯔山遺跡出土

河姆渡遺址博物館蔵

71

敞口釜

T211（4B）:518

高 11.6、口径 26.6 厘米

河姆渡文化一期

1977 年河姆渡遗址出土

河姆渡遗址博物馆藏

***FU* - CAULDRON**

T211（4B）:518

H 11.6 cm　D 26.6 cm（m）

Stage 1 of Hemudu culture

Unearthed from the Hemudu site in 1977

Collected in the Museum of the Hemudu Site

敞口釜

T211（4B）:518

高 11.6 cm　口径 26.6 cm

河姆渡文化 1 期

1977 年河姆渡遺跡出土

河姆渡遺址博物館蔵

72

直口筒腹釜

T226（3A）:16

高 15.4、口径 21.8 厘米

河姆渡文化二期

1977 年河姆渡遗址出土

河姆渡遗址博物馆藏

***FU* – CAULDRON WITH BUCKET BODY**

T226（3A）:16

H 15.4 cm　D 21.8 cm（m）

Stage 2 of Hemudu culture

Unearthed from the Hemudu site in 1977

Collected in the Museum of the Hemudu Site

直口筒腹釜

T226（3A）:16

高 15.4 cm　口徑 21.8 cm

河姆渡文化 2 期

1977 年河姆渡遺跡出土

河姆渡遺址博物館藏

73

扁腹釜

T213（2）:4

高 12.8、口径 20.0、腹径 29.0 厘米

河姆渡文化三期

1977 年河姆渡遗址出土

河姆渡遗址博物馆藏

***FU* – CAULDRON WITH FLAT BODY**

T213（2）:4

H 12.8 cm　D 20.0 cm（m）　D 29.0 cm（body）

Stage 3 of Hemudu culture

Unearthed from the Hemudu site in 1977

Collected in the Museum of the Hemudu Site

扁腹釜

T213（2）:4

高 12.8 cm　口徑 20.0 cm　腹徑 29.0 cm

河姆渡文化 3 期

1977 年河姆渡遺跡出土

河姆渡遺址博物館藏

74
多角沿敞口釜
T222（1）:1
高 22.8、口径 25.2 厘米
河姆渡文化四期
1977 年河姆渡遗址出土
河姆渡遗址博物馆藏

***FU* - CAULDRON**
T222（1）:1
H 22.8 cm　D 25.2 cm（m）
Stage 4 of Hemudu culture
Unearthed from the Hemudu site in 1977
Collected in the Museum of the Hemudu Site

多角沿敞口釜
T222（1）:1
高 22.8 cm　口径 25.2 cm
河姆渡文化 4 期
1977 年河姆渡遺跡出土
河姆渡遺址博物館藏

75
敞口釜
T222（1）:5
高 18.0、口径 25.5 厘米
河姆渡文化四期
1977 年河姆渡遗址出土
河姆渡遗址博物馆藏

***FU* - CAULDRON**
T222（1）:5
H 18.0 cm　D 25.5 cm（m）
Stage 4 of Hemudu culture
Unearthed from the Hemudu site in 1977
Collected in the Museum of the Hemudu Site

敞口釜
T222（1）:5
高 18.0 cm　口径 25.5 cm
河姆渡文化 4 期
1977 年河姆渡遺跡出土
河姆渡遺址博物館藏

76

罐

T242（4A）:313
高 14.0、口径 12.0 厘米
河姆渡文化一期
1977 年河姆渡遗址出土
河姆渡遗址博物馆藏

***GUAN* - JAR**

T242（4A）:313
H 14.0 cm　D 12.0 cm（m）
Stage 1 of Hemudu culture
Unearthed from the Hemudu site in 1977
Collected in the Museum of the Hemudu Site

罐

T242（4A）:313
高 14.0 cm　口徑 12.0 cm
河姆渡文化 1 期
1977 年河姆渡遺跡出土
河姆渡遺址博物館蔵

77

双耳罐

T211（4B）:490

高 17.1、口径 17.4 厘米

河姆渡文化一期

1977 年河姆渡遗址出土

河姆渡遗址博物馆藏

***GUAN* - JAR WITH TWO LOOPS**

T211（4B）:490

H 17.1 cm　D 17.4 cm（m）

Stage 1 of Hemudu culture

Unearthed from the Hemudu site in 1977

Collected in the Museum of the Hemudu Site

双耳罐

T211（4B）:490

高 17.1 cm　口徑 17.4 cm

河姆渡文化 1 期

1977 年河姆渡遺跡出土

河姆渡遺址博物館藏

78

双耳罐

T242（4B）:373

高 15.8、口径 14.0 厘米

河姆渡文化一期

1977 年河姆渡遗址出土

河姆渡遗址博物馆藏

***GUAN* - JAR WITH TWO LOOPS**

T242（4B）:373

H 15.8 cm　D 14.0 cm（m）

Stage 1 of Hemudu culture

Unearthed from the Hemudu site in 1977

Collected in the Museum of the Hemudu Site

双耳罐

T242（4B）:373

高 15.8 cm　口徑 14.0 cm

河姆渡文化 1 期

1977 年河姆渡遺跡出土

河姆渡遺址博物館藏

79

小罐

T213（4A）:122

高 6.5、口径 7.5 厘米

河姆渡文化一期

1977 年河姆渡遗址出土

河姆渡遗址博物馆藏

***GUAN* - JAR**

T213（4A）:122

H 6.5 cm　D 7.5 cm（m）

Stage 1 of Hemudu culture

Unearthed from the Hemudu site in 1977

Collected in the Museum of the Hemudu Site

小罐

T213（4A）:122

高 6.5 cm　口径 7.5 cm

河姆渡文化 1 期

1977 年河姆渡遺跡出土

河姆渡遺址博物館蔵

80

罐

T225（1）:5

高 12.0、口径 8.0 厘米

河姆渡文化四期

1977 年河姆渡遗址出土

河姆渡遗址博物馆藏

***GUAN* - JAR**

T225（1）:5

H 12.0 cm　D 8.0 cm（m）

Stage 4 of Hemudu culture

Unearthed from the Hemudu site in 1977

Collected in the Museum of the Hemudu Site

罐

T225（1）:5

高 12.0 cm　口径 8.0 cm

河姆渡文化 4 期

1977 年河姆渡遺跡出土

河姆渡遺址博物館蔵

81
罐
M9:1
高 11.2、口径 13.2 厘米
河姆渡文化四期
1977 年河姆渡遗址出土
河姆渡遗址博物馆藏

***GUAN* - JAR**
M9:1
H 11.2 cm　D 13.2 cm（m）
Stage 4 of Hemudu culture
Unearthed from the Hemudu site in 1977
Collected in the Museum of the Hemudu Site

罐
M9:1
高 11.2 cm　口径 13.2 cm
河姆渡文化 4 期
1977 年河姆渡遺跡出土
河姆渡遺址博物館蔵

82
罐
M29:3
高 12.2、口径 15.2 厘米
河姆渡文化四期
1990 年塔山遗址出土
象山县文物管理委员会藏

***GUAN* - JAR**
M29:3
H 12.2 cm　D 15.2 cm（m）
Stage 4 of Hemudu culture
Unearthed from the Tashan site in 1990
Collected in the Xiangshan County CPAM

罐
M29:3
高 12.2 cm　口径 15.2 cm
河姆渡文化 4 期
1990 年塔山遺跡出土
象山県文物管理委員会蔵

83

圈足罐
M4:1
高 17.6、口径 12.4、底径 10 厘米
河姆渡文化四期
1989 年名山后遗址出土
奉化市文物保护委员会藏

***GUAN* – JAR WITH RING FOOT**
M4:1
H 17.6 cm D 12.4 cm (m) D 10 cm (b)
Stage 4 of Hemudu culture
Unearthed from Mingshanhou site in 1989
Collected in the Fenghua City CPAM

圈足罐
M4:1
高 17.6 cm 口徑 12.4 cm 底徑 10 cm
河姆渡文化 4 期
1989 年名山後遺跡出土
奉化市文物保護委員会蔵

84

盆

T221（4B）:132
高 12.0、口径 25.0 厘米
河姆渡文化一期
1977 年河姆渡遗址出土
浙江省博物馆藏

***PEN* – BASIN**

T221（4B）:132
H 12.0 cm　D 25. cm（m）
Stage 1 of Hemudu culture
Unearthed from the Hemudu site in 1977
Collected in Zhejiang Provincial Museum

盆

T221（4B）:132
高 12.0 cm　口径 25.0 cm
河姆渡文化 1 期
1977 年河姆渡遺跡出土
浙江省博物館藏

85

鱼藻纹盆

T29（4）:46
高 16.2、口径 30.0 厘米
河姆渡文化一期
1973 年河姆渡遗址出土
浙江省博物馆藏

***PEN* – BASIN WITH FISH AND ALGAE DESIGN**

T29（4）:46
H 16.2 cm　D 30.0 cm（m）
Stage 1 of Hemudu culture
Unearthed from the Hemudu site in 1973
Collected in Zhejiang Provincial Museum

魚藻文盆

T29（4）:46
高 16.2 cm　口径 30.0 cm
河姆渡文化 1 期
1973 年河姆渡遺跡出土
浙江省博物館藏

86

盆

T242（4A）:357

高 14.5、口径 28.0 厘米

河姆渡文化一期

1977 年河姆渡遗址出土

河姆渡遗址博物馆藏

***PEN* – BASIN**

T242（4A）:357

H 14.5 cm　D 28.0 cm（m）

Stage 1 of Hemudu culture

Unearthed from the Hemudu site in 1977

Collected in the Museum of the Hemudu Site

盆

T242（4A）:357

高 14.5 cm　口径 28.0 cm

河姆渡文化 1 期

1977 年河姆渡遺跡出土

河姆渡遺址博物館蔵

87

稻穗纹敛口钵

T221（4B）:232

高 16.8、口径 28.0、底径 16.0 厘米

河姆渡文化一期

1977 年河姆渡遗址出土

浙江省博物馆藏

***BO* – BOWL WITH RICE DESIGN**

T221（4B）:232

H 16.8 cm　D 28.0 cm（m）　D 16.0 cm（b）

Stage 1 of Hemudu culture

Unearthed from the Hemudu site in 1977

Collected in Zhejiang Provincial Museum

稻穗文斂口鉢

T221（4B）:232

高 16.8 cm　口径 28.0 cm　底径 16.0 cm

河姆渡文化 1 期

1977 年河姆渡遺跡出土

浙江省博物館蔵

88

单耳钵

T9（9）:24

高 9.4、口径 16.2 厘米

河姆渡文化一期

1996 年鲻山遗址出土

河姆渡遗址博物馆藏

***BO* - BOWL WITH ONE LOOP**

T9（9）:24

H 9.4 cm　D 16.2 cm（m）

Stage 1 of Hemudu culture

Unearthed from the Zishan site in 1996

Collected in the Museum of the Hemudu Site

單耳鉢

T9（9）:24

高 9.4 cm　口徑 16.2 cm

河姆渡文化 1 期

1996 年鯔山遺跡出土

河姆渡遺址博物館藏

89

单耳钵

T232（4B）:136

高 10.5、口径 13.0 厘米

河姆渡文化一期

1977 年河姆渡遗址出土

河姆渡遗址博物馆藏

***BO* - BOWL WITH ONE LOOP**

T232（4B）:136

H 10.5 cm　D 13.0 cm（m）

Stage 1 of Hemudu culture

Unearthed from the Hemudu site in 1977

Collected in the Museum of the Hemudu Site

單耳鉢

T232（4B）:136

高 10.5 cm　口徑 13.0 cm

河姆渡文化 1 期

1977 年河姆渡遺跡出土

河姆渡遺址博物館藏

90

双耳钵
T212（4B）:84
高 10.9、口径 22.6 厘米
河姆渡文化一期
1977 年河姆渡遗址出土
河姆渡遗址博物馆藏

***BO* – BOWL WITH TWO LOOPS**
T212（4B）:84
H 10.9 cm　D 22.6 cm（m）
Stage 1 of Hemudu culture
Unearthed from the Hemudu site in 1977
Collected in the Museum of the Hemudu Site

双耳鉢
T212（4B）:84
高 10.9 cm　口径 22.6 cm
河姆渡文化 1 期
1977 年河姆渡遺跡出土
河姆渡遺址博物館藏

91

钵

T235（4B）:140

高 9.0、口径 16.0 厘米

河姆渡文化一期

1977 年河姆渡遗址出土

河姆渡遗址博物馆藏

***BO* – BOWL**

T235（4B）:140

H 9.0 cm　D 16.0 cm（m）

Stage 1 of Hemudu culture

Unearthed from the Hemudu site in 1977

Collected in the Museum of the Hemudu Site

鉢

T235（4B）:140

高 9.0 cm　口径 16.0 cm

河姆渡文化 1 期

1977 年河姆渡遺跡出土

河姆渡遺址博物館藏

92

猪纹圆角长方钵

T243（4A）:235

高 11.7、口 21.7×17.5、底 17×13.5 厘米

河姆渡文化一期

1977 年河姆渡遗址出土

浙江省博物馆藏

RECTANGULAR *BO* – BOWL WITH PIG DESIGN

T243（4A）:235

H 11.7 cm　21.7×17.5 cm（m）　17×13.5 cm（b）

Stage 1 of Hemudu culture

Unearthed from the Hemudu site in 1977

Collected in Zhejiang Provincial Museum

豚文円角長方鉢

T243（4A）:235

高 11.7 cm　口部 21.7×17.5 cm　底部 17×13.5 cm

河姆渡文化 1 期

1977 年河姆渡遺跡出土

浙江省博物館藏

93

盘
高 6.8、口径 21.8 厘米
1977 年河姆渡遗址出土
河姆渡遗址博物馆藏

***PAN* – PLATE**
H 6.8 cm　D 21.8 cm (m)
Unearthed from the Hemudu site in 1977
Collected in the Museum of the Hemudu Site

盤
高 6.8 cm　口徑 21.8 cm
1977 年河姆渡遺跡出土
河姆渡遺址博物館藏

94

翻沿盘
T215（4B）:87
高 5.4、口径 30.0 厘米
河姆渡文化一期
1977 年河姆渡遗址出土
河姆渡遗址博物馆藏

PAN **- PLATE WITH EVERTED RIM**
T215（4B）:87
H 5.4 cm　D 30.0 cm（m）
Stage 1 of Hemudu culture
Unearthed from the Hemudu site in 1977
Collected in the Museum of the Hemudu Site

翻沿盤
T215（4B）:87
高 5.4 cm　口徑 30.0 cm
河姆渡文化 1 期
1977 年河姆渡遺跡出土
河姆渡遺址博物館藏

95

六角盘
T34（4）:29
高 5.0、口径 12～18 厘米
河姆渡文化一期
1973 年河姆渡遗址出土
浙江省博物馆藏

SIX LOBED *PAN* - PLATE
T34（4）:29
H 5.0 cm D 12 - 18cm（m）
Stage 1 of Hemudu culture
Unearthed from the Hemudu site in 1973
Collected in Zhejiang Provincial Museum

六角盤
T34（4）:29
高 5.0 cm 口徑 12～18 cm
河姆渡文化 1 期
1973 年河姆渡遺跡出土
浙江省博物館蔵

96

盘	***PAN* - PLATE**	**盤**
T211（4B）:500	T211（4B）:500	T211（4B）:500
高 5.5、口径 24.0 厘米	H 5.5 cm　D 24.0 cm（m）	高 5.5 cm　口径 24.0 cm
河姆渡文化一期	Stage 1 of Hemudu culture	河姆渡文化 1 期
1977 年河姆渡遗址出土	Unearthed from the Hemudu site in 1977	1977 年河姆渡遺跡出土
河姆渡遗址博物馆藏	Collected in the Museum of the Hemudu Site	河姆渡遺址博物館藏

97

圈足盘
M5∶1
高 10.6、口径 16.5 厘米
河姆渡文化四期
1990 年塔山遗址出土
象山县文物管理委员会藏

***PAN* – PLATE WITH RING FOOT**
M5∶1
H 10.6 cm　D 16.5 cm（m）
Stage 4 of Hemudu culture
Unearthed from the Tashan site in 1990
Collected in the Xiangshan County CPAM

圈足盤
M5∶1
高 10.6 cm　口径 16.5 cm
河姆渡文化 4 期
1990 年塔山遺跡出土
象山県文物管理委員会蔵

98
盘形豆
T211（4B）:447
高 10.4、口径 12.0 厘米
河姆渡文化一期
1977 年河姆渡遗址出土
浙江省博物馆藏

PLATE SHAPED *DOU* – STEMMED BOWL
T211（4B）:447
H 10.4 cm D 12.0 cm（m）
Stage 1 of Hemudu culture
Unearthed from the Hemudu site in 1977
Collected in Zhejiang Provincial Museum

盤形豆
T211（4B）:447
高 10.4 cm 口徑 12.0 cm
河姆渡文化 1 期
1977 年河姆渡遺跡出土
浙江省博物館藏

99
豆
T216（4A）:102
高 9.4、口径 14.0 厘米
河姆渡文化一期
1977 年河姆渡遗址出土
河姆渡遗址博物馆藏

***DOU* – STEMMED BOWL**
T216（4A）:102
H 9.4 cm D 14.0 cm（m）
Stage 1 of Hemudu culture
Unearthed from the Hemudu site in 1977
Collected in the Museum of the Hemudu Site

豆
T216（4A）:102
高 9.4 cm 口徑 14.0 cm
河姆渡文化 1 期
1977 年河姆渡遺跡出土
河姆渡遺址博物館藏

100

豆

T243（3B）:197

高 17.4、口径 26.4 厘米

河姆渡文化二期

1977 年河姆渡遗址出土

河姆渡遗址博物馆藏

DOU **– STEMMED BOWL**

T243（3B）:197

H 17.4 cm　D 26.4 cm（m）

Stage 2 of Hemudu culture

Unearthed from the Hemudu site in 1977

Collected in the Museum of the Hemudu Site

豆

T243（3B）:197

高 17.4 cm　口徑 26.4 cm

河姆渡文化 2 期

1977 年河姆渡遺跡出土

河姆渡遺址博物館藏

101
豆
M17:1
高 23.3、口径 19.8 厘米
河姆渡文化三期
1990 年塔山遗址出土
浙江省文物考古研究所藏

***DOU* - STEMMED BOWL**
M17:1
H 23.3 cm D 19.8 cm (m)
Stage 3 of Hemudu culture
Unearthed from the Tashan site in 1990
Collected in Zhejiang Provincial Institute of Cultural Relics and Archaeology

豆
M17:1
高 23.3 cm 口径 19.8 cm
河姆渡文化 3 期
1990 年塔山遺跡出土
浙江省文物考古研究所蔵

102
豆
M29:6
高 14.7、口径 16.6 厘米
河姆渡文化三期
1990 年塔山遗址出土
象山县文物管理委员会藏

***DOU* - STEMMED BOWL**
M29:6
H 14.7 cm D 16.6 cm (m)
Stage 3 of Hemudu culture
Unearthed from the Tashan site in 1990
Collected in the Xiangshan County CPAM

豆
M29:6
高 14.7 cm 口径 16.6 cm
河姆渡文化 3 期
1990 年塔山遺跡出土
象山県文物管理委員会蔵

103

豆

M2:3

高 13.8　口径 18.0 厘米

河姆渡文化四期

1977 年河姆渡遗址出土

河姆渡遗址博物馆藏

DOU **– STEMMED BOWL**

M2:3

H 13.8 cm　D 18.0 cm（m）

Stage 4 of Hemudu culture

Unearthed from the Hemudu site in 1977

Collected in the Museum of the Hemudu Site

豆

M2:3

高 13.8 cm　口徑 18.0 cm

河姆渡文化 4 期

1977 年河姆渡遺跡出土

河姆渡遺址博物館藏

104

豆

M6:3

高 9.0、口径 20.0 厘米

河姆渡文化四期

1977 年河姆渡遗址出土

河姆渡遗址博物馆藏

DOU **– STEMMED BOWL**

M6:3

H 9.0 cm　D 20.0 cm（m）

Stage 4 of Hemudu culture

Unearthed from the Hemudu site in 1977

Collected in the Museum of the Hemudu Site

豆

M6:3

高 9.0 cm　口徑 20.0 cm

河姆渡文化 4 期

1977 年河姆渡遺跡出土

河姆渡遺址博物館藏

105

盂形器
T244（4B）:224
高 7.5、口径 4.5 厘米
河姆渡文化一期
1977 年河姆渡遗址出土
河姆渡遗址博物馆藏

***YU* - SHAPED VESSEL**
T244（4B）:224
H 7.5 cm　D 4.5 cm（m）
Stage 1 of Hemudu culture
Unearthed from the Hemudu site in 1977
Collected in the Museum of the Hemudu Site

盂形器
T244（4B）:224
高 7.5 cm　口腹径 4.5 cm
河姆渡文化 1 期
1977 年河姆渡遺跡出土
河姆渡遺址博物館藏

106

盂形器

T243（4A）:254

高 9.3、口径 18.0 厘米

河姆渡文化一期

1977 年河姆渡遗址出土

河姆渡遗址博物馆藏

***YU* - SHAPED VESSEL**

T243（4A）:254

H 9.3 cm　D 18.0 cm（m）

Stage 1 of Hemudu culture

Unearthed from the Hemudu site in 1977

Collected in the Museum of the Hemudu Site

盂形器

T243（4A）:254

高 9.3 cm　口径 18.0 cm

河姆渡文化 1 期

1977 年河姆渡遺跡出土

河姆渡遺址博物館蔵

107
盂形器
T36（4）:31
高 6.4、口径 6.3 厘米
河姆渡文化一期
1973 年河姆渡遗址出土
浙江省博物馆藏

***YU*－SHAPED VESSEL**
T36（4）:31
H 6.4 cm　D 6.3 cm（m）
Stage 1 of Hemudu culture
Unearthed from the Hemudu site in 1973
Collected in Zhejiang Provincial Museum

盂形器
T36（4）:31
高 6.4 cm　口徑 6.3 cm
河姆渡文化 1 期
1973 年河姆渡遺跡出土
浙江省博物館藏

108
盂形器
T234（4B）:268
高 10.0、口径 5.5 厘米
河姆渡文化一期
1977 年河姆渡遗址出土
浙江省博物馆藏

***YU*－SHAPED VESSEL**
T234（4B）:268
H 10.0 cm　D 5.5 cm（m）
Stage 1 of Hemudu culture
Unearthed from the Hemudu site in 1977
Collected in Zhejiang Provincial Museum

盂形器
T234（4B）:268
高 10.0 cm　口徑 5.5 cm
河姆渡文化 1 期
1977 年河姆渡遺跡出土
浙江省博物館藏

109

盂形器
T24（4）:41
高 8.6、口径 6.0 厘米
河姆渡文化一期
1973 年河姆渡遗址出土
浙江省博物馆藏

***YU*－SHAPED VESSEL**
T24（4）:41
H 8.6 cm　D 6.0 cm（m）
Stage 1 of Hemudu culture
Unearthed from the Hemudu site in 1973
Collected in Zhejiang Provincial Museum

盂形器
T24（4）:41
高 8.6 cm　口徑 6.0 cm
河姆渡文化 1 期
1973 年河姆渡遺跡出土
浙江省博物館藏

110

方盂

T216（4B）:205

高 18.4、口 15.0×15.0、

底 14.0×14.0 厘米

河姆渡文化一期

1977 年河姆渡遗址出土

浙江省博物馆藏

SQUARE *YU* – BASIN

T216（4B）:205

H 18.4 cm　D 15.0×15.0 cm（m）

D 14.0×14.0 cm（b）

Stage 1 of Hemudu culture

Unearthed from the Hemudu site in 1977

Collected in Zhejiang Provincial Museum

方盂

T216（4B）:205

高 18.4 cm　口部 15.0×15.0 cm

底部 14.0×14.0 cm

河姆渡文化 1 期

1977 年河姆渡遺跡出土

浙江省博物館藏

111

桥形纽器盖

T242（4A）:345

高 6.0、盖径 17.5 厘米

河姆渡文化一期

1977 年河姆渡遗址出土

浙江省博物馆藏

LID WITH BRIDGE SHAPED HANDLE

T242（4A）:345

H 6.0 cm　D 17.5 cm（m）

Stage 1 of Hemudu culture

Unearthed from the Hemudu site in 1977

Collected in Zhejiang Provincial Museum

橋形紐蓋

T242（4A）:345

高 6.0 cm　蓋径 17.5 cm

河姆渡文化 1 期

1977 年河姆渡遺跡出土

浙江省博物館蔵

112

器盖

T221(3B):24

高 6.0、盖径 9.0 厘米

河姆渡文化二期

1977 年河姆渡遗址出土

河姆渡遗址博物馆藏

LID

T221（3B）:24

H 6.0 cm　D 9.0 cm（m）

Stage 2 of Hemudu culture

Unearthed from the Hemudu site in 1977

Collected in the Museum of the Hemudu Site

蓋

T221（3B）:24

高 6.0 cm　蓋径 9.0 cm

河姆渡文化 2 期

1977 年河姆渡遺跡出土

河姆渡遺址博物館蔵

113

双飞燕堆纹器盖

T243（3A）:39

残高 7.5、盖径 18.5 厘米

河姆渡文化二期

1977 年河姆渡遗址出土

LID WITH DOUBLE SWALLOWS APPLIQUE

T243（3A）:39

Surviving H 7.5 cm　D 18.5 cm（m）

Stage 2 of Hemudu culture

Unearthed from the Hemudu site in 1977

双飛燕堆文蓋

T243（3A）:39

残高 7.5 cm　蓋径 18.5 cm

河姆渡文化 2 期

1977 年河姆渡遺跡出土

114

器盖
T233（3B）:120
高 11.0、盖径 21.0 厘米
河姆渡文化二期
1977 年河姆渡遗址出土
河姆渡遗址博物馆藏

LID
T233（3B）:120
H 11.0 cm　D 21.0 cm（m）
Stage 2 of Hemudu culture
Unearthed from the Hemudu site in 1977
Collected in the Museum of the Hemudu Site

蓋
T233（3B）:120
高 11.0 cm　蓋徑 21.0 cm
河姆渡文化 2 期
1977 年河姆渡遺跡出土
河姆渡遺址博物館蔵

115

器盖

T216（2）:7

高 10.2、盖径 21.7 厘米

河姆渡文化三期

1977 年河姆渡遗址出土

河姆渡遗址博物馆藏

LID

T216（2）:7

H 10.2 cm　D 21.7 cm（m）

Stage 3 of Hemudu culture

Unearthed from the Hemudu site in 1977

Collected in the Museum of the Hemudu Site

蓋

T216（2）:7

高 10.2 cm　蓋徑 21.7 cm

河姆渡文化 3 期

1977 年河姆渡遺跡出土

河姆渡遺址博物館藏

116
器座
T215（4B）:72
高 16.5、口径 20.8 厘米
河姆渡文化一期
1977 年河姆渡遗址出土
河姆渡遗址博物馆藏

STAND
T215（4B）:72
H 16.5 cm　D 20.8 cm（m）
Stage 1 of Hemudu culture
Unearthed from the Hemudu site in 1977
Collected in the Museum of the Hemudu Site

器台
T215（4B）:72
高 16.5 cm　口径 20.8 cm
河姆渡文化 1 期
1977 年河姆渡遺跡出土
河姆渡遺址博物館藏

117
器座
T212（4B）:155
高 17.0、口径 21.2 厘米
河姆渡文化一期
1977 年河姆渡遗址出土
河姆渡遗址博物馆藏

STAND
T212（4B）:155
H 17.0 cm　D 21.2 cm（m）
Stage 1 of Hemudu culture
Unearthed from the Hemudu site in 1977
Collected in the Museum of the Hemudu Site

器台
T212（4B）:155
高 17.0 cm　口径 21.2 cm
河姆渡文化 1 期
1977 年河姆渡遺跡出土
河姆渡遺址博物館藏

118

方柱形支架
T231（3A）:42
高 17.5、底 9.8×8.1 厘米
河姆渡文化二期
1977 年河姆渡遗址出土
河姆渡遗址博物馆藏

SQUARE POST – SHAPED SUPPORT
T231（3A）:42
H 17.5 cm　D 9.8×8.1 cm（b）
Stage 2 of Hemudu culture
Unearthed from the Hemudu site in 1977
Collected in the Museum of the Hemudu Site

方柱形支脚
T231（3A）:42
高 17.5 cm　底部 9.8×8.1 cm
河姆渡文化 2 期
1977 年河姆渡遺跡出土
河姆渡遺址博物館藏

119

猪嘴形支架
H20:1
高 15.6 厘米
河姆渡文化三期
1977 年河姆渡遗址出土
河姆渡遗址博物馆藏

SWINE'S NOZZLE - SHAPED SUPPORT
H20:1
H 15.6 cm
Stage 3 of Hemudu culture
Unearthed from the Hemudu site in 1977
Collected in the Museum of the Hemudu Site

猪嘴形支脚
H20:1
高 15.6 cm
河姆渡文化 3 期
1977 年河姆渡遺跡出土
河姆渡遺址博物館蔵

120

猪嘴形支架
T18（2）:85
高 16.8 厘米
河姆渡文化三期
1973 年河姆渡遗址出土
浙江省博物馆藏

SWINE'S NOZZLE-SHAPED SUPPORT
T18（2）:85
H 16.8 cm
Stage 3 of Hemudu culture
Unearthed from the Hemudu site in 1973
Collected in Zhejiang Provincial Museum

猪嘴形支脚
T18（2）:85
高 16.8 cm
河姆渡文化 3 期
1973 年河姆渡遺跡出土
浙江省博物館藏

121

拱脊形支架
T242（2B）:11
高 11.8 厘米
河姆渡文化三期
1977 年河姆渡遗址出土

ARC－SHAPED SUPPORT
T242（2B）:11
H 11.8 cm
Stage 3 of Hemudu culture
Unearthed from the Hemudu site in 1977

拱脊形支脚
T242（2B）:11
高 11.8 cm
河姆渡文化 3 期
1977 年河姆渡遺跡出土

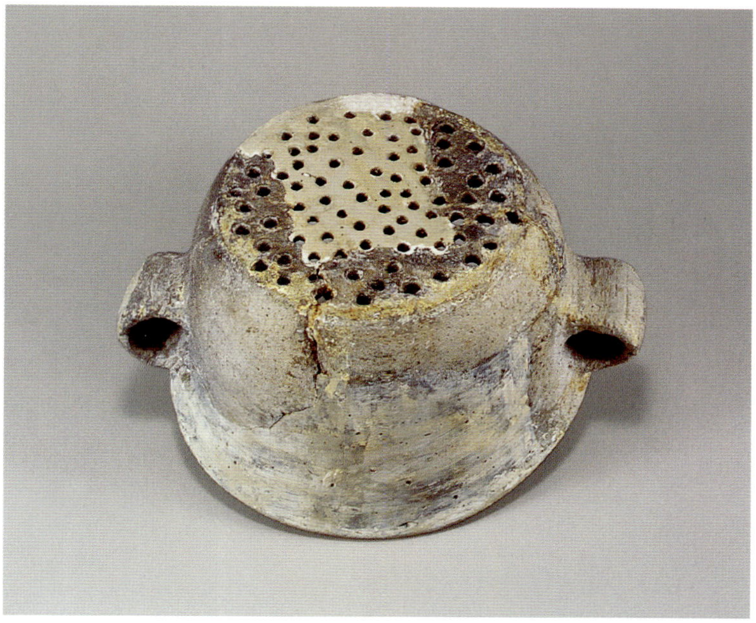

122

甑

T31（3）:8

高 12.4、口径 24.0、底径 14.7 厘米

河姆渡文化二期

1973 年河姆渡遗址出土

浙江省博物馆藏

ZENG **– STEAMER**

T31（3）:8

H 12.4 cm　D 24.0 cm（m）　D 14.7 cm（b）

Stage 2 of Hemudu culture

Unearthed from the Hemudu site in 1973

Collected in Zhejiang Provincial Museum

甑

T31（3）:8

高 12.4 cm　口徑 24.0 cm　底徑 14.7 cm

河姆渡文化 2 期

1973 年河姆渡遺跡出土

浙江省博物館藏

123

灶
T243（3B）:49
残高 25.2、长 54.0 厘米，
底面 28.8×21.5 厘米
河姆渡文化二期
1977 年河姆渡遗址出土
浙江省博物馆藏

STOVE
T243（3B）:49
Surviving H 25.2 cm　L 54.0 cm
D 28.8×21.5 cm（b）
Stage 2 of Hemudu culture
Unearthed from the Hemudu site in 1977
Collected in Zhejiang Provincial Museum

竈
T243（3B）:49
殘高 25.2 cm　長 54.0 cm
底面 28.8×21.5 cm
河姆渡文化 2 期
1977 年河姆渡遺跡出土
浙江省博物館蔵

124

鸟形盉
H21∶3
高 13.2、口径 10 厘米
河姆渡文化二期
1977 年河姆渡遗址出土
河姆渡遗址博物馆藏

BIRD-SHAPED *HE*-ROUND VESSEL
H21∶3
H 13.2 cm D 10 cm (m)
Stage 2 of Hemudu culture
Unearthed from the Hemudu site in 1977
Collected in the Museum of the Hemudu Site

鳥形盉
H21∶3
高 13.2 cm 口徑 10 cm
河姆渡文化 2 期
1977 年河姆渡遺跡出土
河姆渡遺址博物館蔵

125

鸟形盉
H17:3
高 17.9、底径 12.6 厘米
河姆渡文化二期
1996 年鲻山遗址出土
河姆渡遗址博物馆藏

BIRD - SHAPED *HE* - ROUND VESSEL
H17:3
H 17.9 cm D 12.6 cm (b)
Stage 2 of Hemudu culture
Unearthed from the Zishan site in 1996
Collected in the Museum of the Hemudu Site

鳥形盉
H17:3
高 17.9 cm 底徑 12.6 cm
河姆渡文化 2 期
1996 年鯔山遺跡出土
河姆渡遺址博物館藏

126
钵形盉
H3:2
高 10.4、口径 8.8 厘米
河姆渡文化二期
1996 年鲻山遗址出土
河姆渡遗址博物馆藏

BOWL SHAPED *HE* – ROUND VESSEL
H3:2
H 10.4 cm D 8.8 cm (m)
Stage 2 of Hemudu culture
Unearthed from the Zishan site in 1996
Collected in the Museum of the Hemudu Site

鉢形盉
H3:2
高 10.4 cm 口径 8.8 cm
河姆渡文化 2 期
1996 年鲻山遺跡出土
河姆渡遺址博物館藏

127
侧把盉
T12 (7):4
高 12.8、口径 8.0 厘米
河姆渡文化二期
1996 年鲻山遗址出土
河姆渡遗址博物馆藏

***HE* – ROUND VESSEL WITH SIDED HANDLE**
T12 (7):4
H 12.8 cm D 8.0 cm (m)
Stage 2 of Hemudu culture
Unearthed from the Zishan site in 1996
Collected in the Museum of the Hemudu Site

側把盉
T12 (7):4
高 12.8 cm 口径 8.0 cm
河姆渡文化 2 期
1996 年鲻山遺跡出土
河姆渡遺址博物館藏

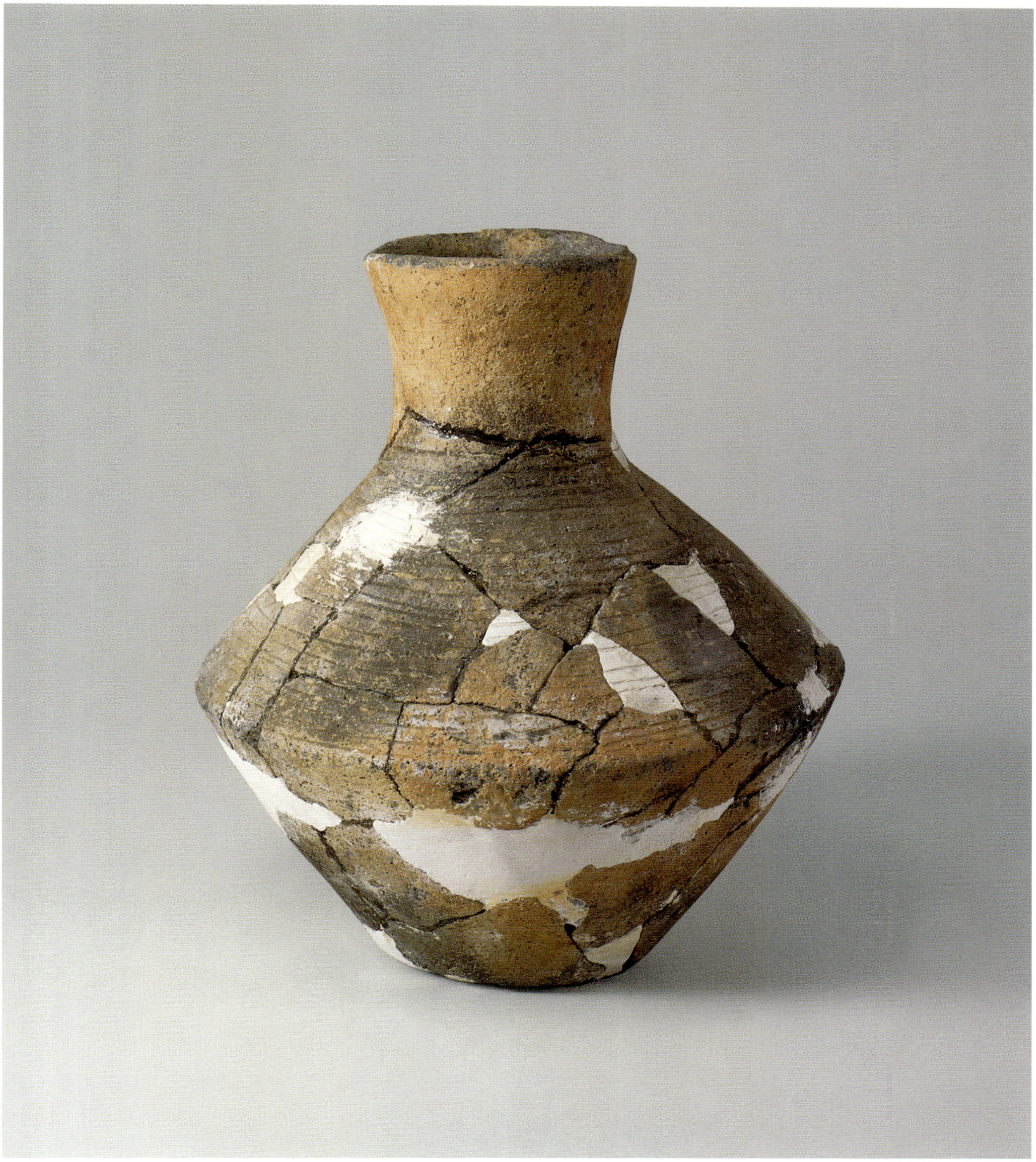

128

壶
M24:3
高 20.5、口径 7.9 厘米
河姆渡文化三期
1990 年塔山遗址出土
象山县文物管理委员会藏

***HU* - POT**
M24:3
H 20.5 cm　D 7.9 cm (m)
Stage 3 of Hemudu culture
Unearthed from the Tashan site in 1990
Collected in the Xiangshan County CPAM

壺
M24:3
高 20.5 cm　口径 7.9 cm
河姆渡文化 3 期
1990 年塔山遺跡出土
象山県文物管理委員会蔵

129

壶	***HU* - POT**	**壺**
M44:4	M44:4	M44:4
高 17.4、口径 7.2 厘米	H 17.4 cm　D 7.2 cm（m）	高 17.4 cm　口径 7.2 cm
河姆渡文化四期	Stage 4 of Hemudu culture	河姆渡文化 4 期
1993 年塔山遗址出土	Unearthed from the Tashan site in 1993	1993 年塔山遺跡出土
象山县文物管理委员会藏	Collected in the Xiangshan County CPAM	象山県文物管理委員会蔵

130

杯

T35（1）:4

高 10.9、口径 6.0 厘米

河姆渡文化四期

1973 年河姆渡遗址出土

浙江省博物馆藏

***BEI* – CUP**

T35（1）:4

H 10.9 cm　D 6.0 cm（m）

Stage 4 of Hemudu culture

Unearthed from the Hemudu site in 1973

Collected in Zhejiang Provincial Museum

杯

T35（1）:4

高 10.9 cm　口徑 6.0 cm

河姆渡文化 4 期

1973 年河姆渡遺跡出土

浙江省博物館藏

131

圈足簋
H23:2
高 12.0、口径 20.4 厘米
河姆渡文化三期
1989 年名山后遗址出土
奉化市文物保护委员会藏

***GUI* – VESSEL WITH RING FOOT**
H23:2
H 12.0 cm D 20.4 cm (m)
Stage 3 of Hemudu culture
Unearthed from Mingshanhou site in 1989
Collected in the Fenghua City CPAM

圈足簋
H23:2
高 12.0 cm 口徑 20.4 cm
河姆渡文化 3 期
1989 年名山後遺跡出土
奉化市文物保護委員会蔵

132

异形鬶

T1514（10）:1

高 17.0、口径 9.2 厘米

河姆渡文化三期

1989 年名山后遗址出土

奉化市文物保护委员会藏

IRREGRULAR－SHAPED *GUI*－PITCHER

T1514（10）:1

H 17.0 cm　D 9.2 cm（m）

Stage 3 of Hemudu culture

Unearthed from Mingshanhou site in 1989

Collected in the Fenghua City CPAM

異形鬶

T1514（10）:1

高 17.0 cm　口徑 9.2 cm

河姆渡文化 3 期

1989 年名山後遺跡出土

奉化市文物保護委員会蔵

133

箕形器
T226（2B）:183
高 9.0、口边长 33.5 厘米
河姆渡文化三期
1977 年河姆渡遗址出土

DUSTPAN－SHAPED WARE
T226（2B）:183
H 9.0 cm　D 33.5 cm（m）
Stage 3 of Hemudu culture
Unearthed from the Hemudu site in 1977

箕形器
T226（2B）:183
高 9.0 cm　口辺長 33.5 cm
河姆渡文化 3 期
1977 年河姆渡遺跡出土

134

釜形鼎
H17:1
高 34.5、口径 34.5 厘米
河姆渡文化三期
1977 年河姆渡遗址出土
河姆渡遗址博物馆藏

CAULDRON - SHAPED *DING* - TRIPOD
H17:1
H 34.5 cm　D 34.5 cm (m)
Stage 3 of Hemudu culture
Unearthed from the Hemudu site in 1977
Collected in the Museum of the Hemudu Site

釜形鼎
H17:1
高 34.5 cm　口徑 34.5 cm
河姆渡文化 3 期
1977 年河姆渡遺跡出土
河姆渡遺址博物館蔵

135
罐形鼎
T231（2B）:22
残高 8.0、口径 8.0 厘米
河姆渡文化三期
1977 年河姆渡遗址出土
河姆渡遗址博物馆藏

JAR - SHAPED *DING* - TRIPOD
T231（2B）:22
Surviving H 8.0 cm　D 8.0 cm（m）
Stage 3 of Hemudu culture
Unearthed from the Hemudu site in 1977
Collected in the Museum of the Hemudu Site

罐形鼎
T231（2B）:22
残高 8.0 cm　口徑 8.0 cm
河姆渡文化 3 期
1977 年河姆渡遺跡出土
河姆渡遺址博物館蔵

136
鼎
H4:8
高 22.6、口径 25.0 厘米
河姆渡文化三期
1989 年名山后遗址出土
奉化市文物保护委员会藏

***DING* - TRIPOD**
H4:8
H 22.6 cm　D 25.0 cm（m）
Stage 3 of Hemudu culture
Unearthed from Mingshanhou site in 1989
Collected in Fenghua City CPAM

鼎
H4:8
高 22.6 cm　口徑 25.0 cm
河姆渡文化 3 期
1989 年名山後遺跡出土
奉化市文物保護委員会蔵

137

带盖鼎
M29∶1
高 16.6、口径 14.0、盖径 13.2、盖高 6.4 厘米
河姆渡文化三期
1990 年塔山遗址出土
象山县文物管理委员会藏

***DING* – TRIPOD WITH LID**
M29∶1
H 16.6 cm D 14.0 cm (m) D 13.2 cm (lid),
H 6.4 cm (lid)
Stage 3 of Hemudu culture
Unearthed from the Tashan site in 1990
Collected in the Xiangshan County CPAM

鼎（蓋付き）
M29∶1
高 16.6 cm 口径 14.0 cm 蓋径 13.2 cm
蓋の高 6.4 cm
河姆渡文化 3 期
1990 年塔山遺跡出土
象山県文物管理委員会蔵

138

埙

T23（4）:46

长 9.0、腹径 5.5、孔径 1.1 厘米

河姆渡文化一期

1973 年河姆渡遗址出土

浙江省博物馆藏

***XUN* – MUSICAL INSTRUMENT**

T23（4）:46

L 9.0 cm　D 5.5 cm（body）　D 1.1 cm（hole）

Stage 1 of Hemudu culture

Unearthed from the Hemudu site in 1973

Collected in Zhejiang Provincial Museum

塤（楽器）

T23（4）:46

長 9.0 cm　腹径 5.5 cm　孔径 1.1 cm

河姆渡文化 1 期

1973 年河姆渡遺跡出土

浙江省博物館蔵

139

兽塑
T223（4A）:106
高 19.0、长 24.0 厘米
河姆渡文化一期
1977 年河姆渡遗址出土

ANIMAL FIGURINE
T223（4A）:106
H 19.0 cm　L 24.0 cm
Stage 1 of Hemudu culture
Unearthed from the Hemudu site in 1977

動物土偶
T223（4A）:106
高 19.0 cm　長 24.0 cm
河姆渡文化 1 期
1977 年河姆渡遺跡出土

140

人首塑

左：T235（3B）:42

高 4.5 厘米

中：T234（3A）:24

高 3.4 厘米

右：T242（3B）:71

高 2.9 厘米

河姆渡文化二期

1977 年河姆渡遗址出土

浙江省博物馆藏

SCULPTURES OF HUMAN HEAD

Left：T235（3B）:42

H 4.5 cm

Middle：T234（3A）:24

H 3.4 cm

Right：T242（3B）:71

H 2.9 cm

Stage 2 of Hemudu culture

Unearthed from the Hemudu site in 1977

Collected in Zhejiang Provincial Museum

人物像

左：T235（3B）:42

高 4.5 cm

中：T234（3A）:24

高 3.4 cm

右：T242（3B）:71

高 2.9 cm

河姆渡文化 2 期

1977 年河姆渡遺跡出土

浙江省博物館蔵

141

人首塑
T30（2）:8
高 4.0 厘米
河姆渡文化三期
1973 年河姆渡遗址出土
浙江省博物馆藏

SCULPTURE OF HUMAN HEAD
T30（2）:8
H 4.0 cm
Stage 3 of Hemudu culture
Unearthed from the Hemudu site in 1973
Collected in Zhejiang Provincial Museum

人物像
T30（2）:8
高 4.0 cm
河姆渡文化 3 期
1973 年河姆渡遺跡出土
浙江省博物館藏

142

小陶玩

左 1：T244（3B）:61（罐）
　　高 4.9、口径 2.9 厘米
左 2：T243（4A）:208（钵）
　　高 2.9、口径 3.8 厘米
中 1：T234（4B）:240
　　高 6.6、口径 6.2 厘米
中 2：T233（4B）:195（陀螺）
　　高 3.5、直径 3.2 厘米
右：T226（3B）:78
　　残长 7.1 厘米
河姆渡文化一、二期
1977 年河姆渡遗址出土
河姆渡遗址博物馆藏

SMALL TOYS

Left 1：T244（3B）:61（*Guan*-Jar）
　　H 4.9 cm　D2.9 cm（m）
Left 2：T243（4A）:208（*Bo*-Bowl）
　　H 2.9 cm　D 3.8 cm（m）
Middle 1：T234（4B）:240
　　H 6.6 cm　D 6.2 cm（m）
Middle 2：T233（4B）:195（Top）
　　H 3.5 cm　D 3.2 cm
Right：T226（3B）:78
　　Surviving L 7.1 cm
Stages 1 and 2 of Hemudu culture
Unearthed from the Hemudu site in 1977
Collected in the Museum of the Hemudu Site

玩具

左 1：T244（3B）:61（罐）
　　高 4.9 cm　口径 2.9 cm
左 2：T243（4A）:208（鉢）
　　高 2.9 cm　口径 3.8 cm
中 1：T234（4B）:240（罐）
　　高 6.6 cm　口径 6.2 cm
中 2：T233（4B）:195（コマ）
　　高 3.5 cm　直径 3.2 cm
右：T226（3B）:78
　　残長 7.1 cm
河姆渡文化 1、2 期
1977 年河姆渡遺跡出土
河姆渡遺址博物館蔵

143
猪
T21（4）:24
高 4.5、长 6.3 厘米
河姆渡文化一期
1973 年河姆渡遗址出土
浙江省博物馆藏

PIG FIGURINE
T21（4）:24
H 4.5 cm　L 6.3 cm
Stage 1 of Hemudu culture
Unearthed from the Hemudu site in 1973
Collected in Zhejiang Provincial Museum

豚形土器
T21（4）:24
高 4.5 cm　長 6.3 cm
河姆渡文化 1 期
1973 年河姆渡遺跡出土
浙江省博物館藏

144
羊形塑
T16（4）:59
高 4.5、长 6.3 厘米
河姆渡文化一期
1973 年河姆渡遗址出土
浙江省博物馆藏

SHEEP FIGURINE
T16（4）:59
H 4.5 cm　L 6.3 cm
Stage 1 of Hemudu culture
Unearthed from the Hemudu site in 1973
Collected in Zhejiang Provincial Museum

羊形土偶
T16（4）:59
高 4.5 cm　長 6.3 cm
河姆渡文化 1 期
1973 年河姆渡遺跡出土
浙江省博物館藏

145
鱼形塑
T242（3B）:68
高 2.0、残长 4.3 厘米
河姆渡文化二期
1977 年河姆渡遗址出土
浙江省博物馆藏

FISH FIGURINE
T242（3B）:68
H 2.0 cm surviving L 4.3 cm
Stage 2 of Hemudu culture
Unearthed from the Hemudu site in 1977
Collected in Zhejiang Provincial Museum

魚形土偶
T242（3B）:68
高 2.0 cm　殘長 4.3 cm
河姆渡文化 2 期
1977 年河姆渡遺跡出土
浙江省博物館藏

146
鸟
T225（3B）:41
高 7、长 8.8 厘米
河姆渡文化二期
1977 年河姆渡遗址出土
浙江省博物馆藏

BIRD FIGURINE
T225（3B）:41
H 7 cm　L 8.8 cm
Stage 2 of Hemudu culture
Unearthed from the Hemudu site in 1977
Collected in Zhejiang Provincial Museum

鳥形土器
T225（3B）:41
高 7 cm　長 8.8 cm
河姆渡文化 2 期
1977 年河姆渡遺跡出土
浙江省博物館藏

147

五叶纹陶块
T213（4A）:84
高 19.5、残宽 18、厚 5.7 厘米
河姆渡文化一期
1977 年河姆渡遗址出土
浙江省博物馆藏

POTSHARD WITH FIVE - LEAF DESIGN
T213（4A）:84
H 19.5 cm surviving W 18 cm T 5.7 cm
Stage 1 of Hemudu culture
Unearthed from the Hemudu site in 1977
Collected in Zhejiang Provincial Museum

五葉文陶塊
T213（4A）:84
高 19.5 cm 残幅 18 cm 厚さ5.7 cm
河姆渡文化 1 期
1977 年河姆渡遺跡出土
浙江省博物館蔵

148

砖形刻纹陶块

T33（4）:90

残高 15.0、残宽 9.0、厚 10.0 厘米

河姆渡文化一期

1973 年河姆渡遗址出土

POTSHARD WITH BRICK DESIGN

T33（4）:90

Surviving H 15.0 cm　Surviving W 9.0 cm　T 10.0 cm

Stage 1 of Hemudu culture

Unearthed from the Hemudu site in 1973

磚形刻文陶塊

T33（4）:90

殘高 15.0 cm　殘寬 9.0 cm　厚 10.0 cm

河姆渡文化 1 期

1973 年河姆渡遺跡出土

149

瓦形刻纹陶片

T33（4）:98

残长 21.4、周残径 13.8 厘米

河姆渡文化一期

1973 年河姆渡遗址出土

浙江省博物馆藏

TILE-SHAPED ARTIFACT WITH DESIGN

T33（4）:98

Surviving L 21.4 cm　surviving D 13.8 cm

Stage 1 of Hemudu culture

Unearthed from the Hemudu site in 1973

Collected in Zhejiang Provincial Museum

瓦形刻文陶片

T33（4）:98

殘長 21.4 cm　殘直徑 13.8 cm

河姆渡文化 1 期

1973 年河姆渡遺跡出土

浙江省博物館蔵

150

彩陶片

左：T211（4B）:523

残高 4.8、残宽 4.4、

厚 0.5 厘米

右：T231（4B）:283

残长 5.5、残宽 4.6 厘米

河姆渡文化一期

1977 年河姆渡遗址出土

河姆渡遗址博物馆藏

PAINTED POTSHARDS

Left：T211（4B）:523

Surviving H 4.8 cm surviving W 4.4 cm

T 0.5 cm

Right：T231（4B）:283

Surviving L 5.5 cm surviving W 4.6 cm

Stage 1 of Hemudu culture

Unearthed from the Hemudu site in 1977

Collected in the Museum of the Hemudu Site

彩文土器片

左：T211（4B）:523

残高 4.8 cm 残幅 4.4 cm

厚さ0.5 cm

右：T231（4B）:283

残長 5.5 cm 残幅 4.6 cm

河姆渡文化 1 期

1977 年河姆渡遺跡出土

河姆渡遺址博物館蔵

木构遗迹

Remains of Wooden Structure

木造建築

河姆渡文化木构遗迹主要是干栏式建筑和水井。干栏式建筑以河姆渡第一、二期文化保存最为丰富和壮观。在河姆渡遗址两次发掘中随处可见密密麻麻的木板和纵横交错的一排排桩木、长圆木，总数达数千件以上。成排的木桩是当时的房屋基础，高出地面 80～100 厘米，说明这是一种居住面悬空的干栏式建筑。房屋的木构件连接除了用藤条捆扎外，还出现了上百件榫卯木构件，有柱头及柱脚榫、梁头榫、平身柱上的卯、转角柱上的卯、带销钉孔榫、燕尾榫、企口板、直棂栏杆和刻花木构件等。

木构水井由 200 余根桩木、长圆木等组成，分内外两部分：外围是一圈直径约 6 米的近圆形的栅栏桩，中心偏西北为边长约 2 米的近方形水井，井壁用四排桩木和 8 根平卧长圆木加固。

The remains of wooden structure recovered in the Hemudu culture mainly consist of pile-dwellings and well. The pile-dwelling structures are richest and magnificent in stages 1 and 2. Extensive remains of wooden columns, piles and base boards were densely arranged, over 1000 pieces of wooden components were unearthed in two excavations. With piles as the base structure about 80-100 cm above the ground, we believe it is a pile-dwelling that was raised above the ground. Of the unearthed articles, about 100 wooden building components were found. They are mainly columns and piles with various types of joints such as dovetail, notched tenon and mortise joints, match boards, balusters and engraved wooden articles. The discovery shows the Hemudu inhabitants had invented tenon and mortise joints besides traditional rattan binding.

The well at the Hemudu site consists of over 200 piles and boards with two parts: the inner and the outer. The outer part is a circle of piles with the diameter of 6 meters, while in the inner part there is a square well with the side as 2 meters long. Four rows of piles and eight horizontal boards made into a square supporting frame of the well to consolidate the frame structure.

河姆渡文化の木造建築遺構は主に高床式建築と井戸である。高床式建築は河姆渡第 1、2 期文化において最も保存がよく壮観である。河姆渡遺跡の2 度の発掘中、随所で密集して木板と縦横に交錯する杭列、丸木が見られ、その数は数千点以上にのぼる。整然と並んだ柱は当時の家屋の基礎であり、地面より 80～100cm 高く、空中に居住面がある高床式建築であることがうかがえる。家屋の木材は藤蔓で縛る以外に、100 点以上の枘・枘穴を持つ木材があり、柱頭枘、柱脚枘、梁頭枘、側柱の枘穴、釘孔を持つ枘、渡腮仕口、実はぎ板、格子欄干と模様を刻んだ木材などがある。

木製井戸は200 本余りの杭、丸木などを組み合わせて作られており、内外両部分に分かれる。外周は一周が直径約 6mほどの円形に近い柵で、内周は中心が西北にやや偏った1 辺約 2mの方形の井戸であり、井戸の壁は4 列の柱と8 本の杙で補強している。

151
第二次发掘木构建筑遗迹
河姆渡文化一期
1977年河姆渡遗址出土

WOODEN STRUCTURE REMAINS OF THE SECOND EXCAVATION
Stage 1 of Hemudu culture
Unearthed from the Hemudu site in 1977

第2次発掘で発見された木造建築遺構
河姆渡文化1期
1977年河姆渡遺跡出土

152
带卯木构件
长 138.0、宽 12.0、厚 11.0 厘米
河姆渡文化一期
1977 年河姆渡遗址出土
河姆渡遗址博物馆藏

WOODEN COMPONENT WITH MORTISE JOINT
L 138.0 cm W 12.0 cm T 11.0 cm
Stage 1 of Hemudu culture
Unearthed from the Hemudu site in 1977
Collected in the Museum of the Hemudu Site

枘穴のある木材
長 138.0 cm 幅 12.0 cm 厚さ11.0 cm
河姆渡文化 1 期
1977 年河姆渡遺跡出土
河姆渡遺址博物館蔵

153
带榫木构件
长 83.0、宽 14.2～15.8、厚 12.0～12.5 厘米
河姆渡文化一期
1977 年河姆渡遗址出土
河姆渡遗址博物馆藏

WOODEN COMPONENT WITH TENON JOINT
L 83.0 cm W 14.2 – 15.8 cm T 12.0 – 12.5 cm
Stage 1 of Hemudu culture
Unearthed from the Hemudu site in 1977
Collected in the Museum of the Hemudu Site

枘のある木材
長 83.0 cm 幅 14.2～15.8 cm 厚さ12.0～12.5 cm
河姆渡文化 1 期
1977 年河姆渡遺跡出土
河姆渡遺址博物館蔵

154
柱头、柱脚榫
T225（4A）:17
河姆渡文化一期
1977 年河姆渡遗址出土

TENONS OF CAPITAL AND FOOT OF COLUMN
T225（4A）:17
Stage 1 of Hemudu culture
Unearthed from the Hemudu site in 1977

柱頭、柱脚の枘
T225（4A）:17
河姆渡文化 1 期
1977 年河姆渡遺跡出土

155
带销钉孔榫
T222（4B）
河姆渡文化一期
1977 年河姆渡遗址出土

TENON
T222（4B）
Stage 1 of Hemudu culture
Unearthed from the Hemudu site in 1977

釘穴のある枘
T222（4B）
河姆渡文化 1 期
1977 年河姆渡遺跡出土

156
燕尾榫
T211（4A）:337
河姆渡文化一期
1977 年河姆渡遗址出土

DOVETAIL TENON JOINT
T211（4A）:337
Stage 1 of Hemudu culture
Unearthed from the Hemudu site in 1977

渡腮仕口
T211（4A）:337
河姆渡文化 1 期
1977 年河姆渡遺跡出土

157
梁头榫
T22:D157
河姆渡文化一期
1973年河姆渡遗址出土

TENON JOINT OF BEAM
T22:D157
Stage 1 of Hemudu culture
Unearthed from the Hemudu site in 1973

梁頭枘
T22:D157
河姆渡文化1期
1973年河姆渡遺跡出土

158
企口板
T18（4）
河姆渡文化一期
1973年河姆渡遗址出土

MATCHBOARD
T18（4）
Stage 1 of Hemudu culture
Unearthed from the Hemudu site in 1973

実はぎ板
T18（4）
河姆渡文化1期
1973年河姆渡遺跡出土

159
木板上的凸榫
T20（4）
河姆渡文化一期
1973年河姆渡遗址出土

CONVEX TENON JOINT OF WOODEN BOARD
T20（4）
Stage 1 of Hemudu culture
Unearthed from the Hemudu site in 1973

板上の凸枘
T20（4）
河姆渡文化1期
1973年河姆渡遺跡出土

160

雕花木构件
YM（4）:木 201
河姆渡文化一期
河姆渡遗址出土

CARVED WOODEN COMPONENT
YM（4）:WOOD 201
Stage 1 of Hemudu culture
Unearthed from the Hemudu site

彫刻のある木材
YM（4）:木 201
河姆渡文化 1 期
河姆渡遺跡出土

161

排桩
河姆渡文化一期
1973年河姆渡遗址出土

ROW OF PILES
Stage 1 of Hemudu culture
Unearthed from the Hemudu site in 1973

柱列
河姆渡文化1期
1973年河姆渡遺跡出土

162

带撑木柱
河姆渡文化二期
1996 年鲻山遗址出土

COLUMN WITH STRUT
Stage 2 of Hemudu culture
Unearthed from the Zishan site in 1996

木柱
河姆渡文化 2 期
1996 年鯔山遺跡出土

163

木构水井

J1

河姆渡文化三期

1973年河姆渡遗址出土

WOOD FRAMED WELL

J1

Stage 3 of Hemudu culture

Unearthed from the Hemudu site in 1973

木造の井戸

J1

河姆渡文化3期

1973年河姆渡遺跡出土

动、植物遗存及其他

Remains of Animals, Plants and Others

動、植物遺存体及びその他

河姆渡特有的自然环境及土壤成分，造就了特别良好的地下保存条件，使得一大批有机物得以保存下来。遗址发现的动、植物遗存数量之多，保存之完好，种属之丰富为国内其他新石器时代遗址所罕见。特别是大面积的人工栽培稻谷遗存和驯养的狗、水牛、猪等骨骸的发现，表明河姆渡文化时期已有了发达的稻作农业和家畜饲养业。同时编织精湛的苇席、绳子的发现，说明当时已有相当先进的编织技术。

The good natural environment and soil components make favorable preservative conditions and a great amount of organic remains preserved well. The wealth of animal and plant remains discovered at the Hemudu site in quantity and species dominates over any other Neolithic sites in China. The remains of cultivated rice found in large area show that the rice agriculture is advance in Hemudu culture. The bone remains of domesticated dogs, water buffaloes and pigs demonstrated that domestic animal husbandry is developed. In addition, the woven reed mat and hand twirled rope indicate the spinning and weaving technique has already reached a high level in Hemudu culture.

河姆渡特有の自然環境と土壌の成分により保存条件が良好であり、有機物が非常によく保存されている。遺跡内から動物遺存体が数量、種類ともに多く、保存もよい状態で発見されることは、国内のその他の新石器時代の遺跡でもまれである。広い面積にわたる人工栽培稲の遺存体と馴化した犬、水牛、豚などの家畜の骨は特別な発見であり、河姆渡文化の時期に発達した稲作農耕と家畜の飼育が行われていたことが分かる。同時に巧みに編まれたアンペラや縄の発見は、当時編み物の技術が相当進んでいたことを物語っている。

164
稻谷
河姆渡文化一期
1977 年河姆渡遗址出土
河姆渡遗址博物馆藏

RICE
Stage 1 of Hemudu culture
Unearthed from the Hemudu site in 1977
Collected in the Museum of the Hemudu Site

稲籾
河姆渡文化 1 期
1977 年河姆渡遺跡出土
河姆渡遺址博物館蔵

165
稻谷堆积
T234（4）
河姆渡文化一期
1977 年河姆渡遗址出土

RICE DEPOSIT
T234（4）
Stage 1 of Hemudu culture
Unearthed from the Hemudu Site in 1977

稲籾の堆積
T234（4）
河姆渡文化 1 期
1977 年河姆渡遺跡出土

166

酸枣

河姆渡文化一期

1977 年河姆渡遗址出土

河姆渡遗址博物馆藏

WILD JUJUBES

Stage 1 of Hemudu culture

Unearthed from the Hemudu site in 1977

Collected in the Museum of the Hemudu Site

サネブトナツメ

河姆渡文化 1 期

1977 年河姆渡遺跡出土

河姆渡遺址博物館蔵

167

橡子

河姆渡文化一期

1977 年河姆渡遗址出土

河姆渡遗址博物馆藏

ACRONS

Stage 1 of Hemudu culture

Unearthed from the Hemudu site in 1977

Collected in the Museum of the Hemudu Site

クヌギ

河姆渡文化 1 期

1977 年河姆渡遺跡出土

河姆渡遺址博物館蔵

168

芡实

河姆渡文化一期

1977 年河姆渡遗址出土

河姆渡遗址博物馆藏

GORGON FRUITS

Stage 1 of Hemudu culture

Unearthed from the Hemudu site in 1977

Collected in the Museum of the Hemudu Site

オニバスの実

河姆渡文化 1 期

1977 年河姆渡遺跡出土

河姆渡遺址博物館蔵

169

樟科叶片
河姆渡文化一期
1977 年河姆渡遗址出土
河姆渡遗址博物馆藏

LEAF OF CAMPHOR TREE
Stage 1 of Hemudu culture
Unearthed from the Hemudu site in 1977
Collected in the Museum of the Hemudu Site

クスノキ科の葉
河姆渡文化 1 期
1977 年河姆渡遺跡出土
河姆渡遺址博物館藏

170
菱角、叶
河姆渡文化一期
1977 年河姆渡遗址出土
河姆渡遗址博物馆藏

WATER－CHESTNUT AND LEAF
Stage 1 of Hemudu culture
Unearthed from the Hemudu site in 1977
Collected in the Museum of the Hemudu Site

ヒシの実、葉
河姆渡文化 1 期
1977 年河姆渡遺跡出土
河姆渡遺址博物館蔵

171
葫芦籽、皮
河姆渡文化一期
1977 年河姆渡遗址出土
河姆渡遗址博物馆藏

SEEDS AND SKIN OF GOURD
Stage 1 of Hemudu culture
Unearthed from the Hemudu site in 1977
Collected in the Museum of the Hemudu Site

ヒョウタンの種、皮
河姆渡文化 1 期
1977 年河姆渡遺跡出土
河姆渡遺址博物館蔵

172

水鹿角

长 41.3 厘米

河姆渡文化一期

1977 年河姆渡遗址出土

河姆渡遗址博物馆藏

ANTLER OF CERVUS UNICOLOR KERR

L 41.3 cm

Stage 1 of Hemudu culture

Unearthed from the Hemudu site in 1977

Collected in the Museum of the Hemudu Site

水鹿（サンバー）の角

長 41.3 cm

河姆渡文化 1 期

1977 年河姆渡遺跡出土

河姆渡遺址博物館藏

173

梅花鹿角

T216（4B）:148

长 17.3 厘米

河姆渡文化一期

1977 年河姆渡遗址出土

河姆渡遗址博物馆藏

ANTLER OF CERVUS NIPPON TEMMINCK

T216（4B）:148

L 17.3 cm

Stage 1 of Hemudu culture

Unearthed from the Hemudu site in 1977

Collected in the Museum of the Hemudu Site

梅花鹿（ニホンジカ）の角

T216（4B）:148

長 17.3 cm

河姆渡文化 1 期

1977 年河姆渡遺跡出土

河姆渡遺址博物館藏

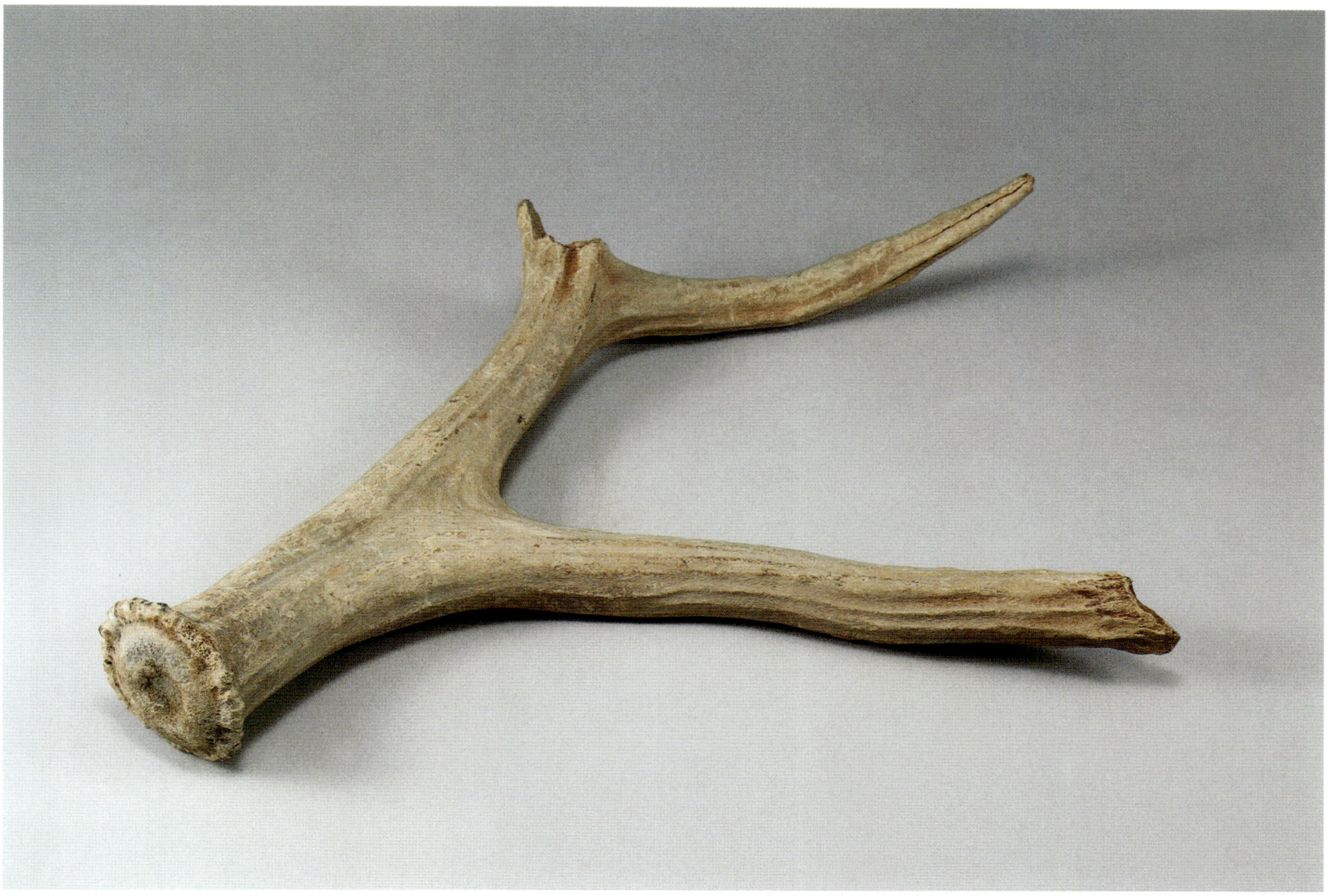

174

四不像角
长 45.0 厘米
河姆渡文化一期
1977 年河姆渡遗址出土
河姆渡遗址博物馆藏

ANTLER OF ELAPHURUS DAVIDIANUS M.
L 45.0 cm
Stage 1 of Hemudu culture
Unearthed from the Hemudu site in 1977
Collected in the Museum of the Hemudu Site

シフゾウの角
長 45.0 cm
河姆渡文化 1 期
1977 年河姆渡遺跡出土
河姆渡遺址博物館蔵

175
左：鸦桡骨
长 14.9 厘米
右：隼肱骨
长 21.1 厘米
河姆渡文化一期
1977 年河姆渡遗址出土
河姆渡遗址博物馆藏

Left: RADIUS OF CROW
L 14.9 cm
Right: HUMERUS OF FALCON
L 21.1 cm
Stage 1 of Hemudu culture
Unearthed from the Hemudu site in 1977
Collected in the Museum of the Hemudu Site

左：カラスの橈骨
長 14.9 cm
右：ハヤブサの翼の骨
長 21.1 cm
河姆渡文化 1 期
1977 年河姆渡遺跡出土
河姆渡遺址博物館蔵

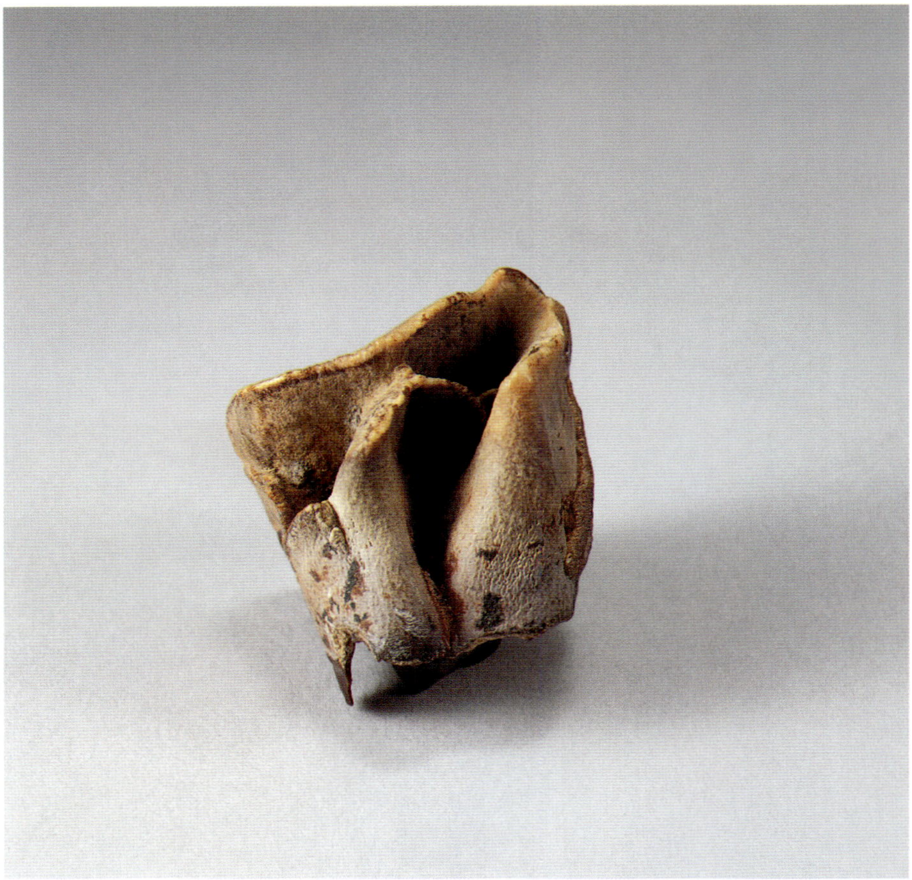

176
犀牛上臼齿
长 5.8 厘米
河姆渡文化一期
1977 年河姆渡遗址出土
河姆渡遗址博物馆藏

UPPER MOLAR OF RHINOCEROS
L 5.8 cm
Stage 1 of Hemudu culture
Unearthed from the Hemudu site in 1977
Collected in the Museum of the Hemudu Site

サイの上臼歯
長 5.8 cm
河姆渡文化 1 期
1977 年河姆渡遺跡出土
河姆渡遺址博物館蔵

177
红面猴下颌骨
长 10.6 厘米
河姆渡文化一期
1977 年河姆渡遗址出土
河姆渡遗址博物馆藏

LOWER JAW OF MACACA SPECIOSA F. CUVIER
L 10.6 cm
Stage 1 of Hemudu culture
Unearthed from the Hemudu site in 1977
Collected in the Museum of the Hemudu Site

ベニガオザルの下顎骨
長 10.6 cm
河姆渡文化 1 期
1977 年河姆渡遺跡出土
河姆渡遺址博物館蔵

178
圣水牛头骨
残高 27.0 厘米
河姆渡文化一期
1977 年河姆渡遗址出土
河姆渡遗址博物馆藏

SKULL OF BUBALUS MEPHISTO PHELES MEPHISTO
Surviving H 27.0 cm
Stage 1 of Hemudu culture
Unearthed from the Hemudu site in 1977
Collected in the Museum of the Hemudu Site

スイギュウの頭骨
残高 27.0 cm
河姆渡文化 1 期
1977 年河姆渡遺跡出土
河姆渡遺址博物館蔵

179

猪下颌骨
长 21.1 厘米
河姆渡文化一期
1977年河姆渡遗址出土
河姆渡遗址博物馆藏

LOWER JAW OF PIG
L 21.1 cm
Stage 1 of Hemudu culture
Unearthed from the Hemudu site in 1977
Collected in the Museum of the Hemudu Site

ブタの下顎骨
長 21.1 cm
河姆渡文化 1 期
1977 年河姆渡遺跡出土
河姆渡遺址博物館蔵

180
貉头骨
长 10.3 厘米
河姆渡文化一期
1977 年河姆渡遗址出土
河姆渡遗址博物馆藏

SKULL OF NYCTEREUTES PROCYONOIDES GRAY
L 10.3 cm
Stage 1 of Hemudu culture
Unearthed from the Hemudu site in 1977
Collected in the Museum of the Hemudu Site

タヌキの頭骨
長 10.3 cm
河姆渡文化 1 期
1977 年河姆渡遺跡出土
河姆渡遺址博物館蔵

181
左：龟头骨
残长 5.5 厘米
右：中华鳖头骨
长 5.8、宽 3.4 厘米
河姆渡文化一期
1977 年河姆渡遗址出土
河姆渡遗址博物馆藏

Left: SKULL OF CHINEMYS REEVESII
Surviving L 5.5 cm
Right: SKULL OF AMYDA SINENSIS
L 5.8 cm W 3.4 cm
Stage 1 of Hemudu culture
Unearthed from the Hemudu site in 1977
Collected in the Museum of the Hemudu Site

左：亀の頭骨
残長 5.5 cm
右：中華鱉の頭骨
長 5.8 cm 幅 3.4 cm
河姆渡文化 1 期
1977 年河姆渡遺跡出土
河姆渡遺址博物館蔵

182

绳索残件

T233（4A）:88

长 23.5 厘米

河姆渡文化一期

1977 年河姆渡遗址出土

浙江省博物馆藏

FRAGMENTS OF ROPE

T233 (4A):88

L 23.5 cm

Stage 1 of Hemudu culture

Unearthed from the Hemudu site in 1977

Collected in Zhejiang Provincial Museum

縄の残片

T233（4A）:88

長 23.5 cm

河姆渡文化 1 期

1977 年河姆渡遺跡出土

浙江省博物館蔵

183

苇席残片
T233（4）
河姆渡文化一期
1977 年河姆渡遺址出土
浙江省博物馆藏

FRAGMENT OF REEDMAT
T233（4）
Stage 1 of Hemudu culture
Unearthed from the Hemudu site in 1977
Collected in Zhejiang Provincial Museum

アンペラの残片
T233（4）
河姆渡文化 1 期
1977 年河姆渡遺跡出土
浙江省博物館藏

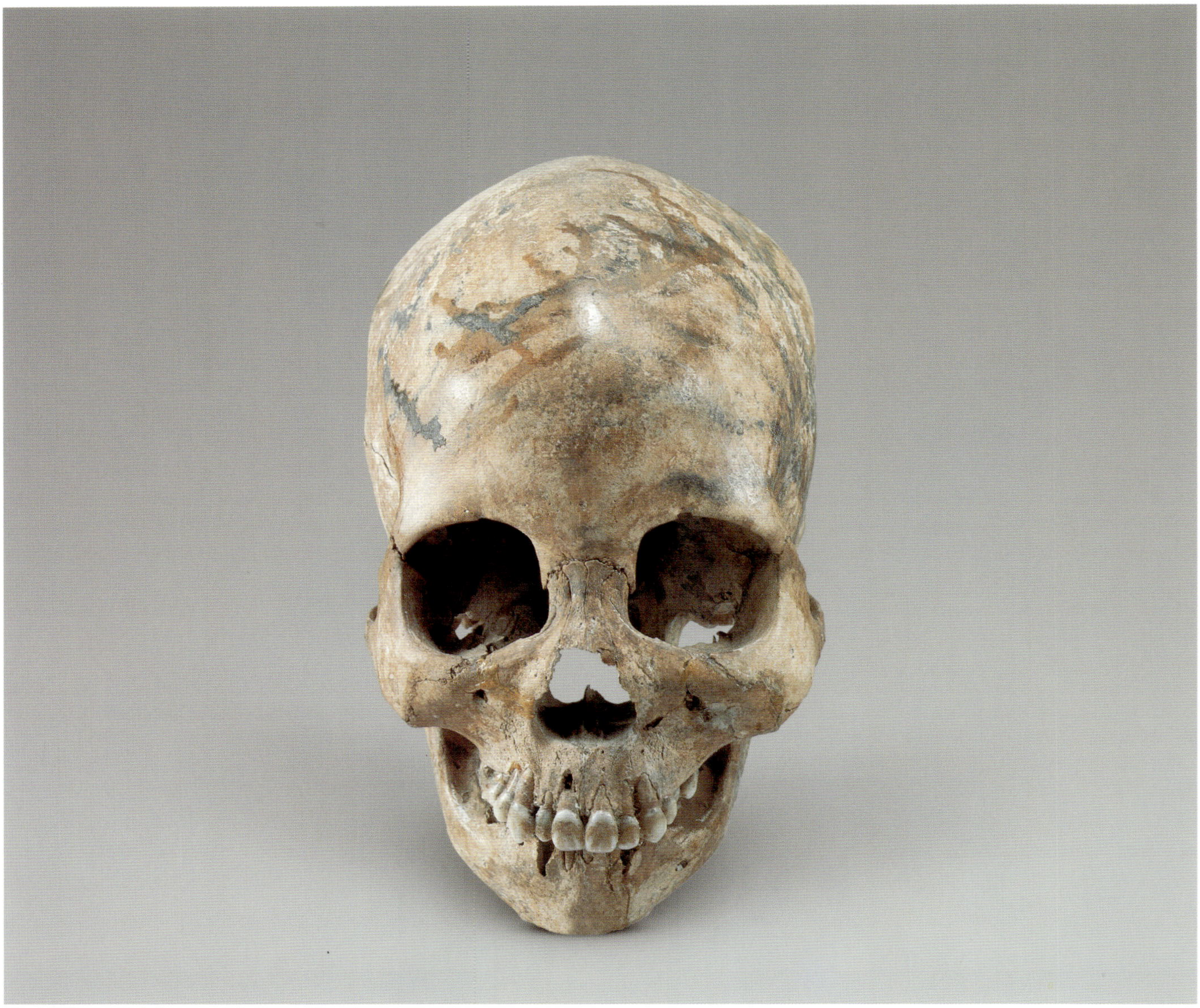

184

女性头骨
M17
河姆渡文化二期
1977 年河姆渡遗址出土
河姆渡遗址博物馆藏

FEMALE SKULL
M17
Stage 2 of Hemudu culture
Unearthed from the Hemudu site in 1977
Collected in the Museum of the Hemudu Site

女性の頭骨
M17
河姆渡文化 2 期
1977 年河姆渡遺跡出土
河姆渡遺址博物館蔵

185

男性头骨

M23

河姆渡文化二期

1977 年河姆渡遗址出土

河姆渡遗址博物馆藏

MALE SKULL

M23

Stage 2 of Hemudu culture

Unearthed from the Hemudu site in 1977

Collected in the Museum of the Hemudu Site

男性の頭骨

M23

河姆渡文化 2 期

1977 年河姆渡遺跡出土

河姆渡遺址博物館蔵

186

鲞架山瓮棺葬
河姆渡文化四期
1994 年鲞架山遗址出土
河姆渡遗址博物馆藏

URN – BURIAL EXCAVATED FROM XIANGJIASHAN SITE
Stage 4 of Hemudu culture
Unearthed from Xiangjiashan site in 1994
Collected in the Museum of the Hemudu Site

鯗架山の甕棺葬
河姆渡文化 4 期
1994 年鯗架山遺跡出土
河姆渡遺址博物館蔵

后　记

河姆渡遗址1973年发现，至今已近30年了，河姆渡遗址博物馆明年也将迎来十周年馆庆。编辑出版一本大型画册，以较全面地反映河姆渡文化的面貌，是我们多年来的夙愿。在中共余姚市委、余姚市人民政府的关怀和市文化局、财政局的支持下，这一愿望终于得以实现，我们备感欣慰。

《河姆渡文化精粹》所录以河姆渡遗址出土的文物精品为主，不少为首次发表，同时还收录了河姆渡文化其他遗址的文物精品。本书由河姆渡遗址博物馆组织编撰。在编写过程中刘军先生悉心指导，并拨冗作序，又同王海明先生一起校阅了部分文字稿，并提供了部分珍贵的图片资料，在此表示衷心的感谢。

本画册的编撰还得到了浙江省文物局、浙江省文物考古研究所、浙江省博物馆、奉化市文物保护委员会办公室、象山县文物管理委员会等单位的大力支持。浙江省博物馆俞为洁女士等为拍摄文物给予了很大的帮助，启功先生为本书题写书名，为画册增色。在此深表谢忱。

由于水平有限，本画册难免有不尽人意之处，敬请专家、读者指正。

编　者

2002年1月

Postscript

It has been 30 years since the first discovery of the Hemudu site in 1973. The Museum of the Hemudu Site will greet her 10th anniversary in the next year. It is a long-cherished wish to compile a large album and to represent the Hemudu culture comprehensively. Under the concern of Yuyao Municapal Commission of Cpc and Yuyao Municapal Government and the support of Yuyao Municapal Bureau of Culture and Yuyao Municapal Bureau of Treasury, we are gratified at the fulfillment of this wish.

The *Gems of the Hemudu Culture* mainly collected cultural treasures from the Hemudu site; many of them are published for the first time. A number of artifacts of fine quality excavated from other sites of the Hemudu culture are also included. This album is organized and written by the Museum of the Hemudu Site. We are debted to Mr. Liu Jun who has devoted himself to the preparation of this album and also written a preface in the midst of pressing affairs. Together with Mr. Wang Haiming, they have proofread a part of the manuscript and present a batch of valuable photos. We are grateful to them.

The preparation of the present album has been generously sponsored by Zhejiang Provincial Bureau of Cultural Relics, Zhejiang Provincial Institute of Cultural Relics and Archaeology, Zhejiang Provincial Museum, CPAM of Fenghua City and CPAM of Xiangshan County. Ms. Yu Weijie, from Zhejiang Provincial Museum has devoted her expertise in photography. We thank Mr. Qi Gong for his autograph, which add beauty to this album.

Editor
January, 2002

後　記

河姆渡遺跡は1973年に発見され、すでにほぼ30年が過ぎた。河姆渡遺址博物館も来年で開館10周年を迎える。大判の図録を出版し、全面的に河姆渡文化の内容を紹介することは、我々の長年の望みであった。中国共産黨余姚市委員会、余姚市人民政府の配慮と市文化局、財政局の支援のもと、ついに実現するにいたり、感謝の念に耐えない。

『河姆渡文化精粋』に収録されているのは河姆渡遺跡出土の逸品が主で、初めて発表されるものも少なくなく、同時に河姆渡文化のその他の遺跡の逸品も収録している。これは河姆渡遺址博物館が組織的に編纂を行った。執筆過程中、劉軍先生が熱心に指導され、時間を割いて序文をいただき、また王海明先生と共に文字原稿を校正され、貴重な図版資料を提供していただいた。ここに記して感謝の意を表す。

この図録の編纂にはさらに浙江省文物局、浙江省文物考古研究所、浙江省博物館、奉化市文物保護委員会辦公室、象山県文物管理委員会などの機関の強力な支持を得た。浙江省博物館の兪為洁女士などには遺物撮影に大変ご協力頂いた。啓功先生には本書の書名の題字を書いていただき、非常に光栄である。ここに深くお礼申し上げる。

力に限りがあり、この図録には足りない所も多いが、どうか研究者、読者の方々にご指導いただきたい。

編集者

2002年1月